MW00439754

Last of the Old-Time Texans

Mackey Murdock

Republic of Texas Press
Plano, Texas

Library of Congress Cataloging-in-Publication Data

Murdock, Mackey.
  Last of the old-time Texans / Mackey Murdock.
     p. cm.
  Includes index.
  ISBN 1-55622-784-1
  1. Texas—Biography. 2. Texas—Social life and customs—20th century.
  3. Texas—History, Local. 4. Interviews—Texas. 5. Murdock, Mackey.
  I. Title.

  CT262 .M87 2000
  920.0764—dc21   00-038703
                                    CIP

© 2000, Mackey Murdock

All Rights Reserved

Republic of Texas Press is an imprint of Wordware Publishing, Inc.
No part of this book may be reproduced in any form or by
any means without permission in writing from
Wordware Publishing, Inc.

Printed in the United States of America

ISBN 1-55622-784-1
10 9 8 7 6 5 4 3 2
0004

All inquiries for volume purchases of this book should be addressed to
Wordware Publishing, Inc., at 2320 Los Rios Boulevard, Plano, Texas 75074.
Telephone inquiries may be made by calling:

(972) 423-0090

Contents

Author's Note

A friend suggested I write the story of the last of the old-time Texans.

Images of mentors, friends, and loved ones passed in review as I categorized their timeframe. The earlier members of such a group would have entered the twentieth century as adolescents, and the later members plucked victory from defeat during World War II.

Having missed the old-timer class by only a decade or two, I jumped at the idea. I've always held their accomplishments and sacrifices in awe, marveled at their stories, and admired the nobility of their character. More, I revere their friendship. Perhaps, having missed their road brand only a few years, my earmarking will allow me the honor of bringing up the drag and recording a few of their yarns while highlighting portions of their life.

Their trail isn't hard to locate. Unlike their parents, the early Texans, this stock left plenty of sign. They built things. The trick for me is to avoid mussing up the tracks they laid.

Even after they're penned, culling a herd is a chore. Matching the gender, age, and size is generally turned over to a top hand. A sense of pride, a feeling of honor welled from within. I thought of the task ahead. Where mavericks are going (in this case where they've been) determines the alley to head them for and the gate to close. Thinking of the bunch I wanted, I chose to go for the grandfathers and grandmothers who act as the corner post of the fence our life strands tie to. The ones set deep and straight and dug by hand.

Concerned with how to delimit the book, I thought of a gentleman with old-time roots who coached what some called "God's Team" in Dallas. Certainly, he'd make any Texas list. Still, others from our state went to the White House or made big generals or both. The city of Houston even claims some moon walkers had a Lone-Star connection. Since most of us live beyond the glaring light of celebrity, I chose to avoid these headliners.

I am indebted to hundreds of storytellers, officials, club members, and other interested parties who saw the need a quarter-century ago to get their county's stories told and, in so doing, preserved a treasure of factual information concerning these truly noble people. Many of these contributors are no longer with us. Interviewing those I found was a privilege. In general, I've attempted to keep this their story, flavored with their words.

In addition to the dozens of personal interviews conducted in creating this book, I've drawn on a lifetime of informal memories of shared times spent with old-timers. A short biography of twenty-eight representative members of this era, under the heading of "Old-Timer's Tally Sheet," graces the book's final chapter. Sixteen of its members are alive today and contributed significantly to this book by interviews while twelve others emerged from research of Texas county histories. These folks, plus hundreds of their contemporaries, provide both the grain and the fodder sandwiched between these covers.

To preserve their earthy and colorful way of storytelling, I have chosen to let them speak for themselves and, to this end, have taken only limited liberty in editing their words. Unless identified otherwise by state name, sites referenced are in Texas. Efforts to verify the spelling of proper names at times ended with fading memories. Corrections brought to my attention will be incorporated in later editions of this book.

Old-Timer's Vernacular

Annie godlin—(noun-adjective), a diagonal line or course.

Blind bridle—(noun), a bridle fashioned with a leather extension around the eye to restrict rear vision.

Boot—(noun), additional items committed to balance a trade.

Brakes—(noun), broken and eroded land.

Buck hay—(verb), to load hay.

Dally—(noun), one or more wraps around a saddle horn with rope end opposite the thrown loop.

Doozie—(noun), top of the line, number one, desirable.

Cowboying—(verb), performing the work of a cowboy.

Catty cornered—(noun-adjective), a diagonal line or course.

Dead man—(noun), a rock, post, or other anchor buried near and attached to a corner fence post to steady it.

Fresno (slip)—(noun), a large dirt moving scoop drawn by draft animals.

Empty wagon—(noun), talks like an . . . (rattles).

Gee—(interj.), a right turn command to a draft animal.

Go-devil—(noun), a sled plow with runners and long knives, used to weed young row crops.

Hand—(noun), one who assists or helps, an employee, laborer.

Haw—(interj.), a left turn command to a draft animal.

Head-maize—(noun), maize grown for feed prior to modern milo maize. (verb), to harvest maize by hand.

Hooraw—(verb), to tease good-naturedly.

Laid-by—(noun), crop cultivation and care completed until harvest.

Land—(noun), a marked or distinct area.

Nose twitch—(noun), a rope or chain loop on the end of a stick used to manage a stubborn or frightened horse.

Pert—(adjective), saucy, bold; in good health.

Point row—(noun), the short rows, centered between terraces and connecting with longer contoured rows.

Bank run—(noun), the event of depositors removing their accounts from a bank.

Stomp lot—(noun), a small enclosure, lot, or corral. An enclosure for stock awaiting use (so named because of the frequency of animals stamping at biting flies).

Sulky plow—(noun), a two-wheeled plow with a seat for the rider.

Tight—(adjective), describes soil heavy with clay.

Top-off—(verb), the act of riding the initial ride of the day on a semi-broke horse.

Turn row—(noun), a bare strip in cultivated fields used for turning teams or tractors, generally near fences.

Witching—(verb), divining for underground water or buried material, usually performed with a green forked branch.

Facing the Abyss

$H$is pickup's radio announcer described the blast as unimaginable then supplied details of horror in Oklahoma City. Eighty-five-year-old J. T. "Jake" Murdock shook his head and got out to open the gate. Stepping back to the cab of his truck, there was no way for him to know he faced an even more immediate and personal disaster.

The view from the windshield of the twenty-year-old pickup showed deep, drop-off washes. Devilishly scrambled badlands of rugged bluffs, arroyos, and clay ridgelines extended to the distant cottonwood-lined banks of West Texas's Brazos River. A barbed-wire fence skirted the edges of these gorges. It separated the brakes from plowed farmland.

Jake gave the view only a passing glance. He had a pickup to unload. Inside the pasture, he put the truck in reverse then focused on the rearview mirror. From long practice, his huge hands handled the wheel. He dodged stumps and rocks, backing toward one of the deeper gullies. After fifty years on a piece of land, you know its features. If prior to those years you spent thirty-five gathering the wherewithal for its down payment, chances are you've developed a work ethic that puts first things first.

Jake had such a sense of priority. He also had an arthritic back that made the rearview mirror preferable to twisting to see behind him. Forty years earlier doctors told him time and a back-brace corset would allow nature to calcify the vertebra and free him of most of the pain. The problem was the time was measured in decades. Back pain makes tractor seats, saddles, and bales of hay formidable enemies. Wrapped in one corset after the other, he "sweated out" the years and the sixteen-hour days. Seldom, now, did pain make him grab something to keep from going to his knees.

J.T. "Jake" Murdock, age 50 at time of photo (taken 1960).

He braked the truck leaving enough room to navigate behind the open tailgate to unload the cuttings he'd hauled from his city home in Seymour. He set the emergency brake and got out and stretched.

The old man's broad six-foot-three-inch frame had weathered down to two hundred pounds. There were shallow, hollow crevices running the length of his neck. Silver hair showed beneath the sweatband of his feed-store cap, and his square face showed wrinkles. His jaw line sagged slightly. Still, an air of self-confidence exuded from the man. A faint shadow of sadness covered by determination flitted about the mouth. Though he was in his element, this place also represented what had been home to his young family so many years ago.

Asked, his eyes would shine as he told you in detail how he made and used the first truck semi-trailer west of Fort Worth, Texas. His favorite stories held mostly warmth and laughter. Grown from farm britches too short, he'd hired out at fourteen, married at eighteen, and stayed hitched.

Blessed with good health, he enjoyed a rich life. His first away-from-home job was road building, then farm laborer, gin-hand, trucker, merchant, farmer, and cattleman. Able to make a living at sale barns on other's mistakes, stockmen sought him out to buy for them. He'd deny giving much thought to being one of the last of the old-time Texans but would readily admit to missing a lot of old friends.

Formed from a day when numbers were for math and names for identity, his barefoot years were spent in the piney woods of East Texas. His family brought him west when he was an adolescent, and my mother, and a chance to prove himself, kept him there.

Dad made short work of the unloading and headed for home. He passed through the gate, got out and closed it, then grabbed his chest in pain. The world went black and he swirled in a cyclone of excruciating pain. Sweat ran down his face and his chest seemed to explode. His arms hurt. He knew what was happening. Ten years earlier his wife suffered similarly in his arms. She had not recovered. His son had received six heart bypasses soon after. Jake staggered to the pickup and slumped inside.

Waves of pain tore at him. He put the truck in gear, accelerated down the spinning road—time—he hadn't much time and the nearest hospital was seventeen miles away at Seymour. Fighting the wheel to stay between the ditches, he realized he must go slowly. He yawned and leaned back trying to get air. He got nothing, only a rocklike obstruction in his throat.

If he made it to town he'd go straight to the hospital. Lora, his wife of eight years would be home, but someone could call her. He sensed the ride smooth and realized he'd reached the blacktopped farm-to-market. The fog before him closed, and the truck bounced on the rough shoulder at the edge of the road. He struggled and righted the truck.

Fuzzy figures appeared in a nearby field, near the outline of a vehicle, wagon, tractor, pickup, he wasn't sure. Should he stop for help? No, no time, he struggled on, hurting. Alternately swerving on and off the road between blackouts, he reached town, became confused. People were everywhere. He remembered the parade. Somehow he managed to drive his way through the crowd and stopped a few feet in front of the hospital entrance.

Dad got out of his pickup, stumbled, steadied himself, and staggered into the hospital lobby.

"Mr. Murdock, what's wrong," a nurse yelled.

"I'm having a heart attack!" He collapsed.

I stood by his bed in the little cubicle that served as intensive care in Seymour's good country hospital. The time was near midnight. A nurse sat nearby. Dad slept peacefully. I remembered this was the room my mother died in. I sensed a bond to this nurse, a stranger. Dad's fist held the top of his sheet. He looked small and gray curled there in bed. I noticed those thumbs, still twice as broad as mine, short, squared at the ends. His eyes opened.

Dad adjusted the oxygen harness to his nose. "I told them to call the law down there at Jacksboro and tell him to stop you and tell you to slow down. Tell you I'us doing OK."

"You can never find those guys when you need them," I answered. "You alright?"

"Yeah, I know now what you meant about being so weak, though."

"Dad, I was just standing here thinking that I told more lies in a shorter time in a place like this than any other time in my life."

"What do you mean?"

"Intensive care, the first time I was there I bargained with God all night. Told him if he'd just let me live I'd never smoke again. Seven or eight years later, I was back on them, the biggest liar in Texas."

"Uh huh," Dad smiled peacefully and went back to sleep.

The nurse whispered, "The doctor gave your dad that new shot. You know the one that breaks up clots. They've had good luck with it when administered early enough."

"I'm not familiar with it."

"Normally its not given to patients his age; it's pretty severe, but sometime it does miracles."

The next morning an ambulance carried my father to Wichita Falls. Shortly after our arrival at the hospital, the doctor came out and asked to talk to the family. My stepmother, my wife, and I locked eyes on the man's face.

"Mr. Murdock your father has had an extremely dangerous heart attack. He's eighty-five, and most, even younger, men fail to survive what he's been through. I asked him about artificial life support, you know heroic measures. He said his son was out here and could make that decision for him. It's important we know the answer before action is required. Think about it and let me know in the next few minutes. I'll be back."

It worked out the doctor never learned my decision. We talked the next day. I say talked, mostly the doctor shook his head. "It beats all I ever saw. Had I not had access to the electrocardiogram and been monitoring him during the ordeal, I'd have a hard time proving the man suffered a heart attack. He's got a long way to go, but I'd say his chances now are as good as anyone's."

It's late summer 1999 as I write this. Dad is doing fine. He'll be ninety in January. I'm trying to get him to quit mowing the two yards he has in Seymour. If he will, maybe I'll not be too embarrassed to hire mine done. He's one old-timer who's come a long way. Come to think of it, so has the medical profession.

Born Too
Early

Ethel Glover Ryder, raised on a ranch in Knox County, is typical of the stock that made later-day Texas more people friendly. She titled this story "My Paul Revere Ride." She related it many years ago for the writers of the *Knox County History*.

"'Ethel! Ethel, wake up, quick. Dress warm and ride over to the Reeds' for help. Mother is having that baby, and I can't get the doctor or anyone else on the phone.'

"It was two o'clock, November 1, 1913. I was fourteen, and we lived on the Shawyer Ranch, later known as the Masterson Ranch. The Reeds lived two miles across the fields. I ran to the barn, grabbed my bridle, and raced in the dark, passing fifteen stalls before getting to my horse. On the way back, I grabbed my saddle and ran out of the barn so that I could saddle him in the moonlight where it wasn't so spooky.

"As I swung up, Father yelled, 'Ride as you've never ridden before and don't spare the quirt. There is one baby here and another almost!'

"He needn't have urged me, for soon I discovered one of the night's shadowy Halloween witches riding with me, long hair flying and the brushy end of her broom stretching from under her cape. No matter how much I used the quirt, every time I looked toward the ground, there she was riding neck and neck with me. I was afraid to get off my horse to open the gate, so I slipped the loop, letting the gate fall, then galloped over it.

"Before I reached the neighbors, I was yelling so they came rushing out. The Reeds, Ryders, and Dr. Beaver, from Benjamin, finally got there, but we already had our twin boys. Later we learned that the telephone exchange at Truscott had burned that night."

Ethel's words carry the spirit and energy, the pragmatism so prevalent in the generation of Texans that bore this state into the twentieth century. Yet, beneath the surface, that wonderful humor mixed with a thirst for adventure invited us to share the wind kissing her face as she hurtled through the darkness, her heart in her throat.

The seriousness of her life-and-death mission is but a single task in the array of responsibilities shouldered by all members of the old-time Texas families. The window of opportunity for survival opened only narrowly, and in this land where distances were great and doctors few, children were often called on for tasks demanding Herculean effort.

Randall County historians state, "Sickness was a problem. If the sick person did not respond to simple remedies, they knew there was little left to do but pray. Babies came without benefit of doctors. The women would deliver one another's babies, cut the cord, and take care of mother and baby.

"Mrs. Gordon Cummings, a delicate, frail-looking woman, delivered all three of her children herself, sat up in bed and washed them the best she could. The doctors always arrived too late."

LaVern Cummins, daughter of early Haskell County's doctor D. L. Cummins, adds, "for many years medicine was strictly home talent. The superstitions and remedies that the slaves had as their African heritage were passed on to the family. These mixed with the master's remedies brought from the 'old states.'"

A Collin County old-timer agreed with LaVern, stating that, "The efficient housewife had a home remedy for practically every ailment. Some of the remedies came from the Indians and others from accidental experiences and observations. Boils were often treated with slices of fat meat or with a poultice, sometimes made from peach-tree leaves. Wounds were soaked in kerosene or turpentine, and in case of severe bleeding, soot was added. Sulfur and molasses was the universal 'spring tonic' and was also used for sore throats."

The lady added, "To keep germs away, a small bag of asafetida was worn on a string around the neck—probably effective because its odor kept everybody at a distance. The night air was thought to be harmful; so houses were kept as tightly closed as possible."

Mrs. Juanita Daniel Zachry resided in Taylor County at the turn of the twentieth century. She stated, "In Mulberry Canyon in the late 1890s, Mrs. Sam Butman Sr. was bitten by a rattlesnake. Those with her immediately applied a salve, kept for use on snake-bitten sheep. Dr. Gardner of Merkel came and split the wound several times. Mrs. Butman's leg had extreme swelling and she was ill for weeks, but recovered."

Juanita continued, "A common treatment for poisonous bites and particularly rabies, was the use of the 'mad-stone.' This was a small calcified, porous substance, usually oval-shaped, said to be found in the stomach of animals. Because of the porosity of the mad-stone, it readily absorbed liquid. It was first placed in a pan of warm water or milk then applied to the affected part. If the stone stuck (according to legend), the wound definitely held poison. Early residents say the absorbed liquid often turned green, indicating the poison being drawn out. When it no longer stuck to the wound all the poison was thought withdrawn."

The McKinney *Enquirer* of March 3, 1883, carried this news item. "Isaac F. Graves, his wife and two colored servants were bitten a few days since, by a puppy, afterwards supposed to have rabies. Fearing evil results, they repaired to the mad-stone to have it applied." Sadly, the fate of these victims is unknown.

Mrs. Zachry listed these additional remedies. "The lowly poke weed, which grows profusely in Taylor County, was eaten as a green and called 'poke salet.' The water in which it boiled was used for skin irritations and rashes. The roots of the sprawling red root weed were boiled and used for diarrhea. The bark of the live oak also served the same purpose. The outer fiber was peeled away and the tender inner bark brewed to make a tea. Dried leaves of the mullien plant were smoked by asthma sufferers and said to bring relief."

Earlier John Larkin of Collin County, whose father was a doctor, wrote to a cousin in Illinois saying: "Mother desires you to send her Grandfather's receipt for the salve for curing cancer (the polk salve)."

Whiskey was regarded as the great "cure-all" against everything from the common cold and "la grippe" (influenza) to snakebite. The snake-oil salesman enticed the last coin from many gnarled and callused hands with concoctions bottled in patent medicine bottles and diluted with whatever was handy then scented with strong syrups.

An old-time Wood County cough remedy called for "Rockhound Bone Set and Sutterfly Root in one half gallon of water boiled down to a quart. Strain, add equal honey, simmer until water is gone then add a pint of Codelia and bottle." Usage directions were noted: "take as much as you can bear without vomiting three times a day."

With neighbors sometime scarce, towns scattered, and cities with hospitals almost nonexistent, the sight of a horse and buggy heralding the arrival of a medical man with knowledge, regardless of how limited, must have brought tears of relief to the eyes of many.

The lonely distances presented danger to the physician also. Speaking of her father, Mrs. Cummins said, "One night when Dr. Cummins was making a call on horseback, he was accosted by bandits. Pretending to think it was a prank, he shouted, 'I don't have time to fool with you boys,' he spurred his horse and dashed on. After that experience he carried a pistol in his pocket. One evening, about dusk, he was standing at the front gate talking to a patient who had driven to consult the doctor. Dr. Cummins, hand in pocket, accidentally pulled the trigger.

"Horse and buggy" doctor
Photo courtesy Texas State Library and Archives Commission

"The patient and his wife made a hasty getaway, and seeing the bullet-torn trouser leg, the doctor thought himself ready for medical aid. Fortunately, he didn't need it, as his leg was scarcely grazed. That cheap-enough lesson ended his pistol totin'."

LaVern Cummins validates the period philosophy of making do with what was at hand by adding, "On one occasion, George and Nelson Walton were hastily summoned to the scene of a fight, where they found a man lying split open with his viscera lying outside his body. The Waltons washed off the intestines, replaced them, and sewed the victim up with a spaying needle and some sort of thread. Of course, the patient recovered and, no doubt, fought again."

On occasion the nature of the illness exceeded the bounds of acceptable modesty. LaVern continued, "In taking a call to relay to Papa, I asked the young man calling about the nature of his illness. He stumbled a bit before he said, 'Well, family trouble.' I didn't know whether there had been a shooting or a knifing or a beating.

"I called the telephone operator and she very cordially agreed to step across the street and have Papa call home.

"Speaking of the young father who called, Papa's comment was, 'I've not been paid for his delivery, yet.' But, of course, he went on to usher in the first of a new generation."

The last decade of the 1800s passed then the first seventeen years of the 1900s. Still, the absence of good general medical care, particularly maternal, and the shortage of remedies and those to prescribe them, left the woods, the hills, and the prairies crowded with crosses and headstones.

Adults fell in the prime of their lives, often to rise no more. In some families it was difficult to find adults old enough to determine aging traits such as gray hair and wrinkles. Parents talked of living children and mourned others. No one chaffed more at this unacceptable situation than those noble men with the small valises who spent lonely, often exhausting hours going from one hopeless case to another.

War raged overseas, and armies of men traveled the oceans. The healthy moved to the dying fields of Europe and the maimed and wounded back to the states. As the European smallpox had earlier decimated the Native American population, now influenza prepared to do the same with all in Texas.

Dr. Fred Tarpley wrote of the early Jefferson area. "The winter of 1918-1919 brought a severe influenza epidemic to Jefferson that gave soldiers overseas concern for the welfare of their families on the home front. A volunteer quarantine settled over the town as the number of fatalities increased.

"Jefferson's Chastain family felt the import of the epidemic in a number of ways. Millard Filmore Chastain was an employee of the Haggard Furniture store, which also offered undertaking service. He reported that citizens were dying so fast, so many relatives were bedfast with the flu themselves, and the disease so highly contagious that many victims were buried without funeral services. Joe Chastain left his mother's house without any symptoms of the influenza, but the next day he was dead from the unpredictable virulent strain that few Jefferson families were able to escape."

Juanita Zachry carried the story of early medical treatment back west, toward Abilene. "The lack of medical help and proper knowledge was painfully demonstrated in Potosi in 1893. In the middle of the day, Mrs. Emily (Bob) Pollard became ill with severe abdominal pain and vomiting. All family remedies failed to cool her temperature or relieve the pain. The doctor was at Tye, a distance of fifteen miles.

"Bob Pollard had many fine spirited horses, which were swift runners. He dared not leave his wife, but sent a neighbor boy, Will Nesmith, for the doctor.

"He instructed Will not to spare the horse. 'Run him as long as he'll run, but bring back the doctor.'

"Will told later that he did, in fact, road founder the horse, and it was never of value later. He sent the doctor on ahead to Mrs. Pollard alone as he was without a usable mount. Mrs. Pollard could not be helped. She died of a ruptured appendix at age thirty-nine."

Mrs. Quida Reid, daughter of J. Ben Campbell, at Merkel, remembers Dr. Crawford mixing his own prescription at the patient's bedside. "He would add to the mixture, shake the bottle then turn it up and taste it. This troubled my mother when he did this at our house. She considered it unsanitary, but felt less apprehensive about giving the medicine since he had tasted it."

Dr. W. V. Crawford practiced medicine at Buffalo Gap for many years following his arrival in 1887. The doctor crusaded for progress and took a dim view of the years prior to 1922, which he called "the good old days."

"'I used to ride thirty or forty miles across country, without even a path, to see a patient,' he said in a 1923 interview. 'Sometimes it took two or three days to make a trip. I've spilt open more cold nights than any man in the county. I never want to go back to the old days. I'm thankful for automobiles and other modern conveniences, and the only regret I have is that I lived a hundred years too soon.'"

Dr. Crawford and other residents of Taylor County got their first hospital at Abilene in 1904, but apparently, in his view, progress in the state of the medical art waited until sometime after 1922 to advance from the old days.

The noble doctor joined many others from varied occupations in finding those days difficult and frustrating. The draining grief of being alone or, perhaps, aided by a frightened husband or marginally skilled midwife during a normal childbirth must have brought many to face tomorrow with dread. Those experiencing the frequent tragedy of birth gone wrong or child death from simple illness, no doubt, added to the vast numbers who faced the future with hope and the past with sadness. The loss of loved ones from common disease added to the unforgiving nature of the times. Fatigue sapped the hardiest physique and stooped the strongest frame. Still, hope drove these folks forward—hope that they would make the path easier for those following.

Woven with despair, this glimmer of optimism added meaning to the good doctor's rounds and soothed the pained joints of those adding their labor to the building process. A Bible held a place of reverence in most every home, its worn pages interpreted, its message argued but largely embraced. The description of the workday as being "from can till can't" did not refer to visibility, but rather the worker's strength. It meant rising when rested enough to raise one's head, then working until too tired to lift one's hand. The days started before and extended beyond light. More than one bale of cotton was picked by moonlight. Through all of this a zest for life and humor carried these remarkable people forward with a smile more often than a frown. When the smile became too heavy, the West still beckoned.

Plowed Furrow to School

Before it became Knox County, to the drovers, the buffalo hunters, and the army it was the Knox Prairie. Its grass grew knee-high to a fifteen-hand horse. To the south and west stretched short-grass country, but here the sandy soil held what little moisture fell and converted it to fodder containing ample minerals. Animals foraging on it produced strong bones and heavy muscles.

In the greener and more wooded country to the east, settlements had dotted Texas for years, sometimes generations, but this was maiden land, untouched by plow. Earlier, the Kiowa and Comanche claimed it but did not disturb it. Unable to subdue these warriors in battle, the army destroyed the Indians' mounts. Following shortly after this, hide hunters slaughtered the buffalo. Dismounted and starving, with no choice but forced confinement on reservations, the proud Kiowa and Comanche moved to Indian Territory.

Trail drivers then ranchers were next on the scene. Railroads extended westward and soon, weathered by only a few seasons, the last of the drovers' trails vanished. Upon viewing this grassland, roving homesteaders, gifted with an eye for productive earth, moistened cracked lips and smiled.

Such a man was M. A. Jackson, and on that fertile land he settled. The year was 1889. The fledgling county was in its third year. Like other early arrivals, he and his family lived for a time in a half-dugout. They later moved a mile west and built a house on two hundred acres. Antelope ranged the grassland and there were no trees to hamper a plow.

West Texas, including the rolling and high plains, did not share East Texas's problems with clearing timber. Harvey Moore, a citizen of the timbered country around Jefferson, remembered. "Always a selling point was land cleared of timber, ready for farming. 'Cleared land,' however, did not mean cleared of stumps, a menace to farmer and freighter alike.

"Oxen and mules, pulling plows to break the new ground, strained at the traces, but stumps and roots often seemed more numerous than plants in the row crop. 'The old mule would press hard on the collar and stop dead in his tracks with a grunt and a groan every time the plow hit a stump. The jolt caused the handle to hit me in the groin. I'd grab myself, lean forward, and writhe in pain. Then I'd pull the plow from the stump and start again....Sometimes I was hit with both handles when the plow struck an angling root and sent it across two rows with me trying to catch it.'"

John Bates's grandfather J. H. Bates was an early settler in Knox County. Arriving in 1886 and with an eye for both grass and farming land, he found timber-free virgin prairie. Stumps were less an issue than water with Mr. Bates. He chose land that lay near Lake Creek. John stated, "he bought a claim to section six from W. M. Gulick," an earlier cattleman. "J. H. Bates gave Mr. Gulick a wagon, a span of little mules, and $125 for the section."

Further west, Randall County historians wrote, "About ten years after the ranchers came, the settlers began coming to the Plains. By this time, much of the choicest watered lands along the surface streams had been taken by the cattlemen and cowboys."

Today, Mrs. Nova Schubert Bair is an eighty-eight-year-old poet and former music teacher. She taught at the Amarillo Musical Conservatory for many years. A covered wagon traveler and remuda wrangler in her youth in Hansford County, she stated, "many a second-son from the old country came to the plains of Texas to build their lives."

My ignorance of the significance of second sons must have shown.

"In Europe the first son inherits the nobility, most if not all the property, and most other matters of consequence. Many of the second sons came to the Texas Panhandle to invest or start anew," she explained.

Knox County lies east of the High Plains and the Cap Rock and hence felt the plow a few years prior to that country. It would be another decade, in some cases another generation, before the homesteader moved to the high plains and the desert areas to its southwest. Texas, like a giant field, was being cultivated east to west.

John added, "The Bates moved into a house the former owners had built." The wives of these men, "Mrs. Gulick and Mrs. Colthrop, lived in a half-dugout and used the house as a parlor for company."

Dugouts and half-dugouts were to the earlier settlers what teepees were to the Indians in this dry, treeless country. Dug into the side of a slope, the depth of the dig was the main difference between the newcomers' different structures. The half-dugout had a short wall (siding) of logs, rocks, or sawed lumber extending from outside ground level to the roof line. Deeper, the standard dugout avoided wall construction but had the disadvantage of offering no location for a window to provide light or ventilation. Both structures had a roof of supporting planks or logs and were covered by sod.

Being beneath ground level offered some protection from both heat and cold. The leaves of yucca offered good waterproofing to the roof when matted over and between the supporting timbers then covered with the soil. These were not structures that man or woman wanted to grow old in, but they provided shelter when necessity rather than convenience ruled.

Half-dugout and resident, circa 1909 (West Texas)

Photo by Erwin E. Smith "Judge Henry H. 'Paint' Campbell, original manager and founder of The Matadors, standing before the door of the Matador line camp that served as its first headquarters, Matador Ranch, Texas." Glass plate negative, 1909. LC.S6.224. Courtesy of the Erwin E. Smith Collection of the library of Congress on deposit at the Amon Carter Museum, Fort Worth, Texas.

A few miles to the south, at Ample, Texas, "Mrs. W. P. (Elizabeth) Phillips was appointed postmistress in 1895. The post office was one large room with a loft for a bedroom and a dugout for a kitchen."

Though the transition from state lands to counties took years, in some cases decades, their development followed similar patterns. The appointment of a county or commissioners court was an early act. "Once the county was organized a court was appointed," writes Knox County's historians. Its records show the court voted $2,000 to build a jail in 1887 and then assigned a group to locate sites and build bridges across the Brazos and Wichita Rivers.

Claims were established and deeds recorded and state lands were sold. Schools were a priority. The location, construction, financing, and management of these houses of learning were taken seriously by the entire community.

Well, perhaps the quest for knowledge was more serious on the part of some participants than others. Support sometimes came from unlikely sources. It is said that the T Anchor (T̲) cowboys were generous in subscribing to funds to build the first schoolhouse of Canyon, Texas. To some that seemed strange, since practically all of them were unmarried. The motive became more understandable when a note came out in the *Tascosa Pioneer*, September 27, 1890. "Canyon City has some eighteen or twenty young men and old bachelors and only two young ladies. Come west, young ladies, come west."

Haskell historians wrote, "Life in our community in the last of the nineteenth century was not for the faint-hearted. Children walking to school through cedar brakes could hear the chilling cry of panthers that seemed close. Rattlesnakes infested the area."

The urgency for constructing education facilities can be seen in the following quote from the *Knox County History* showing schools were built before roads. John Bates wrote, "On opening day of school at old Goree North, Bud Holt came to the schoolhouse with a sulky plow and plowed a furrow across the prairies to the Lawson Place. This furrow was for his children to follow in crossing the prairie." Without landmarks and being a distance of four miles, Mr. Holt's concern for his children staying on course is understandable.

These early schools were normally one- to three-room buildings. Frequently a partition separated the cloakroom from the seated students and provided privacy for removing and hanging up winter clothing, headgear, and overshoes.

Large cast-iron stoves provided heat in the winter months. The heavy stoves were generally shielded by lighter weight metal. This covering wrapped around the hot sides to prevent burns. Taller than all but the oldest students, the shield made an excellent place to warm lunches and heat soup.

Coal was the preferred fuel. By the time the last old-time Texans got to school, most found a coal bin or building on the grounds. Being assigned to take the scuttle out for a bucket of coal was a privilege of good citizenship. While the cloakroom offered an opportunity to bump against members of the opposite gender, the coal shed provided a chance to test one's physical might against male companions. Fetching coal was man's work. Girls were more often assigned to dusting erasers.

Carl Nicholson attended elementary school at Oakwood, back in the century's teen years. "If teachers had been paid time-and-a-half for the time they stayed with pupils after school, my teacher would have gotten rich. Looking back, it seems I must have stayed late five days a week.

"What amazes me now is that I managed to escape the lash of the switch. Corporal punishment was allowed in schools in those days and teachers in Oakwood took full advantage of the opportunity. Boys in my age group wore knickers that reached just below their knees and most came to school barefooted on warm days. The teacher's favorite spot for applying the switch was on the bare calf of the student's legs. Many times, I saw boys leave the room with bleeding legs. Occasionally a girl would fall victim of the switch."

Subjects were basic. Emphasis was on the three R's, but some might be surprised at the variety of subject matter. Music, drama, and foreign language were not overlooked. A single teacher commonly had several classes, all in the same room, working on different subjects and levels at one time. Still three or four classes might only account for less than twenty students.

Collin County historians remembered, "Early school games did not include ball, instead pupils played town ball, dare base, rooster fight, hoops, bull pen, crack-the-whip, anti-over [Anne-Over], leap frog, and races."

Jake Murdock explained town ball. "We didn't play with a regular baseball, but rather a smaller hard-rubber ball. We hit it with a flat board and if the fielder caught the ball in the air or on its first hop the batter was out. If you threw the ball between the base runner and the base he was going to he was also out."

Paul Carter remembers playing a game called Peggy when he was a child. "We played Peggy with a three-foot-long stick and a shorter ten-inch or so stick that had a pointed end. We placed the short stick on a fulcrum similar to a seesaw. The idea was to hit the end of the short stick that pointed skyward with the longer stick. The short twig would fly end-over-end and land on its point and stick up. Well, sometimes it would stick up. Anyway, the opponent would have to guess how many steps it would take to retrieve the short stick."

Suddenly, Paul's face took on a stricken look. He couldn't remember if the object of the contest had been to make the short stick fly farther than your opponent or if the accuracy of estimating the steps for retrieval determined the winner.

Residents at Rochester wrote of their school. They remembered a two-story brick building. "On April Fool's day the school authorities did not turn out school, and several boys got in the auditorium at recess and nailed the doors to with a plank so no one could enter. Finally the superintendent sent for the boys' fathers. Trapped on the second floor inside the building, the boys cut the ropes from the curtains, tied them to a chair, and lowered one member safely to the ground. However he, along with the others, suffered the consequences meted out by the angry parents.

"In later years a windmill and tank provided water for faucets that you could turn on and get a drink. Earlier, water was out of a container." Some schools had hand pumps piped to multiple drinking faucets on the playgrounds, and a buddy system was required to get a drink.

"Boys wore heavy jackets, heavy knee-length trousers, and heavy stockings for outside basketball as falling was a little rough. The girls also had excellent basketball teams and wore blouses, large bloomers, and heavy stockings."

Bill Mann attended one of those old-time schools in the 1920s. He was raised in and around Waco. In 1999 we talked. It had been over seventy years since he learned a little poem in school. Mr. Mann had recently been featured on a Dallas TV station for his dedication to comrades who had fallen in defense of our country.

Mann religiously raises and lowers the flag over a portion of a Waco cemetery dedicated to veterans. He made about one dollar the day he and his outfit hit Omaha Beach in WW II in front of the main invasion at Normandy. He gets, and asks for, nothing for his care of the flag.

Bill said, "I learned a little poem way early on in school that has stayed with me, and I try to live by it. I think it was called 'For Others.' It went something like this:

An old man going a lone highway,
came at the evening cold and gray
to a chasm vast—deep and wide.
The old man crossed in the twilight dim,
but the sullen stream had no fear for him.
He turned once safe on the other side
and built a bridge to span the tide.

Old man, said a fellow Pilgrim near,
you're wasting your strength with your building here.
Your journey will end with the ending day.
You never again will pass this way.

The builder lifted his old gray head and
said, good friend, in the path I've come today,
there followeth after me

a fair-haired youth whose feet
must pass this way.
And this chasm which has been naught to me
to that fair-haired youth may a pitfall be.
Good friend I'm building this bridge for him."

There seems little question that Bill learned, and his school taught, at a high level. Bill lacked only one year finishing school when he joined the navy at age seventeen.

William L. "Bill" Mann.
My vote as the most important representative of the era.

Nova Bair was one of those fortunate old-time Texans who continued her education on to a Bachelor's degree. Concerning the area of higher education and proud of her linkage through teachers directly back to Beethoven, she said, "Earlier, in the arts, prestige went from teacher to student as well as from school to student."

Few from this period, particularly in the rural areas where transportation was difficult, completed high school. Large families demanded one support oneself at an early age. Important as school was thought to be, the fifth or sixth grade saw the end of most students' class time.

W. D. Hines continued his schooling for twelve years near Bryan. "The country schoolhouse sat across the fence from the field where Daddy worked. After school, I'd just crawl under the fence and go to work."

Although M. A. Jackson settled in Knox County in 1889, it would be forty-eight years and two generations later before the first of his descendents would be privileged to graduate from high school. As the youngest daughter, Goldia achieved this goal and reached a level of formal education none of her six siblings matched. By the late 1940s many of the next generation were attending college.

A big break for school attendance came in the 1940s with entry of the school bus into the education process. Prior to that time poor roads and worse methods of transportation prevented many traveling to a point where the higher grades were taught. Earlier, students living in rural areas often boarded with someone in nearby towns to attend high school. Better roads and the availability of buses made high school more attainable.

What the schools were too modest to teach, life on the buses took care of. Regimentation remained on the school grounds, and anarchy, socialism, and democracy held sway dependent upon the mood of the day. Social issues were resolved at the whim of the peer group one moment, and the brawn of the biggest participant the next. No doubt a few criminal lessons got an early start on the giant yellow cruisers of the back roads, but we learned a little about self-government.

I remember a driver whose poor eyesight forced him from all other employment so he accepted a job driving the bus. Thinking to get even with our parents and society in general for endangering our safety, we took care of him. We helped by telling him when he was meeting cars and other trivia. In areas where the roads were particularly sandy or narrow he would sometime pull to one side and wait for the other vehicle to pass. On occasion he was given false information, and after spending a lot of time stopped beside the road with no traffic, he seemed to lose confidence in student input. He continued, in wet weather, to off-load bigger boys to push the bus through slick spots when the wheels failed to get traction. Behind the bus and out of sight of his rearview mirrors we could normally have him in the ditch in minutes.

Taking the bus to high school (for a few years elementary schools continued in the rural communities) takes place at about the time a youngster is most keen on learning things not in the books. It's strange how one remembers things that happened on that bus and recalls nothing from the classroom.

The practice of closing rural schools during the harvest season so all could go to the fields and work continued into the era of World War II. For most Texans of this period, mechanization meant a riding plow or a windmill. The fields, the shops, and the homes were built and maintained with physical labor provided by the whole household. The demand for earning a living brought early maturity, and childhood passed swiftly.

In the Fields

Prior to the 1940s even Texans residing in towns and cities lived a life-style similar to their rural counterparts. Merchants stayed rooted to the land, caring for gardens and the family milk cow. Chickens scratched behind each house, and turkeys from an Oak Cliff residence made up Clyde Barrow's first loot.

In East Texas, communities supplemented farm income with railroad work, coal mining, and the lumber industry. In the southern part of the state and along the coast, fishing added its own special flavor to living with the elements, but the land still reigned. Along the Rio Grande, fruit orchards developed into a crop of choice. In West Texas, farms blended with the cattle industry and gradually took over the better land, leaving the rougher and/or timbered areas for grazing.

Though crops and methods differed throughout the state, the need for both a "cash" and a "feed" crop formed a common bond. Cotton, wheat, and in some places, sugarcane and tobacco filled the need for cash. Corn, maize (milo), hay, and bundle feed (sorghum) satisfied the need for a feed crop. Due primarily to rainfall, maize and bundle feeds were grown in the West, and corn and hay were more suited for East Texas feeds.

Farming West Texas's sandy lands, at its best, melded man and nature toward a single goal. Frequently, however, this harmonic relationship turned adversarial. After spring planting, the farmer often found himself in a war, fighting the wind and blowing sand to save his young stand of tender plants from total destruction. Neither forest fires nor herds of stampeding cattle brought economic ruin swifter than the blinding blast of searing sand that annually threatened the early farmer. When conditions were ripe for this disaster, seconds were precious. Minutes of raging sand often destroyed months of preparation.

A few days after planting, the rich, sandy loam is bare, mulched into loose furrows, bedded, row after row, with only the green of tender sprouts showing above ground. Heavy spring rains melt this loose soil, then as it dries it sears and crusts into a glassy, smooth surface. Beneath this thin crust is often mud, but on top the slightest breeze picks up grains of sand and sweeps them down the long rows.

Storm fronts sweep across the plains in the springtime, and many a farmer, even today, sits with his tractor bogged to its axle in mud, watching helplessly while blinding sand strips the land of his fledgling crop. His only chance is to free his equipment and stir the crusted land with harrow or rotary plow to expose not sand, but mulched clods of damp earth to the killer winds. Time and the storm front are his enemies.

One old-timer of this Plains area answered to a nickname. The details of the acquisition of his new name are rooted in one of these warlike situations involving an early 1920s sandstorm. Only a boy of ten or so years, this youngster had been blessed with a strong father, but damned by a romantic fun-loving intelligence that some might describe as more artistic and curious than practical. Music, the flight of birds, and a desire to find something to fill a gnawing need for expression interested him more than oncoming clouds. Supplying him with a team and a section harrow, this boy's father assigned him the man-size job of helping to fight the impending sandstorm threatened by a rapidly approaching "blue norther."

The old man started with a team on one side of a half-section (320 acres) of vulnerable cotton and sent the boy to the other side of the "land." The task consisted of walking behind or, in the case of a small boy, riding a board fastened on top of the harrow while traveling up and down the rows, stirring the crusted soil.

After hours of manning his post and having saved a good portion of the cotton field, "Banjo's" mind began to dwell on things cool, pleasant, and not necessarily related to horses' rumps. Sand stung his eyes when he faced the wind, then drifted damagingly down the unprotected rows of cotton.

A state rooted in agriculture
Photo courtesy Texas State Library and Archives Commission

Across the field his father appeared and disappeared behind gusting sand with each fluctuation of the wind. Big and strong, leaning forward, walking into the wind, following the matched bays, somehow the father seemed smaller measured against the oncoming storm. It would take only a few minutes to walk over there. The wind sighed, and the distant thunder produced a low rumble. The harness creaked. He wished he could make such sounds. He wished he had a banjo.

With no further thought he stopped his team, wrapped the lines around a lever on the harrow, and began to trot to where his father worked. He would hurry. It'd only take a minute—well only a few.

The big man saw him coming, stopped, and waited, hands on hips. "What's wrong?" he asked as the boy approached.

"Daddy, would you buy me a banjo?"

The big man cursed then pointed at the distant team. "Git."

The boy lowered his head. He'd never heard his father curse.

Exasperated, the older man later told the story. It spread. Banjo grew to manhood without his instrument, but he had a firm nickname that followed him to his grave.

Sandstorms ravaged whole sections of the nation during the dust-bowl days of the twenties and early thirties. Clouds of soil blowing in the air hid the sun and turned day into twilight. Chickens went to roosts at midday, and paint was blasted from both wood and metal.

No house was tight enough to hold out the drifting dust. Ladies learned to set tables with the plates and glasses placed upside down until actually in use, then after washing, store them in the same position. Fences were buried when drifting sand clung to weeds along fence lines. Posts appeared to grow downward, and stock walked to freedom.

Those living on the tight lands of black gumbo and red clay were spared much of this risk. Flood, humidity, and insects replaced their western neighbors' sandstorms. Mechanical equipment and more modern farming methods tilted the battle in favor of the farmer, but still, neither exhaustion nor schedule nor time of day excuses those who live where sand blows and conditions are right for it to walk.

Cotton grows well in just about every area of Texas that provides enough water. Nova Bair claims one exception. "The Canadian River, in the Panhandle, divides the north plains from the south plains. The canyons and brakes that accompany this river form a dividing line for the growth of cotton. It does not grow on the north plains, but does well south of there."

Cotton fruition occurs similar to that of fruit trees. The bud is called a "square" and is followed by a white bloom. Levi Strauss and Company is said to be the cotton farmer's best friend, but at this point in its development other friends, like the honeybee, take over and pollinate the plant. The flower turns progressively pinker until a small boll appears at its base. The bloom dries and falls away.

The earlier bolls, found lower on the stalk, mature first then the higher ones take turns cracking open and exposing the fluffy white lint. After the first freeze, when its stalks are dead, bare of leaves, and the last mature bolls are opened, the sun's rays reflect across fields of snowbank white.

Perhaps even more significant than the improvement in working crops has been those in its harvesting. The horse-drawn sickle mower replaced the scythe, then, according to the Collin County historians, the harvesting of wheat, oats, and barley received another advancement. "The stationary thresher, operated by a steam engine and employing a crew of fifteen to twenty men, came into use in the county in the late 1880s and was continued until after 1900.

"During this time, farm women competed with each other in feeding the harvest crews, as farmers exchanged help during the threshing season. Some thresher men operated independently; that is, the owner of the machine fed his own crew from a cook shack.

"In spite of the long hours of back-breaking work, the reward was considered great when the workers sat down to one of those lavish meals. This era of agriculture development has been considered by some old-timers as the most romantic period in all farm history."

Norris Curtis remembered those good thresher meals. "You come in out of that sun, your clothes would be wet with sweat. After you washed up and sat down, somebody would always say, 'Be careful, that iced-tea will make you sick, hot as we've been.'"

Cotton, maize, and corn continued to be gathered strictly by hand until years later. During the era of the plantations, cotton was picked at harvest time. In the earlier days baskets were used as containers for picked cotton. As the term implies this technique required the lint, including the seed, to be plucked or picked from the cotton burr. As cotton gins improved in their ability to clean cotton and remove trash and burrs from the lint, the harvesting method simplified to pulling the cotton boll from the stalk with burr, seed, and lint together. Ginned, two thousand pounds of pulled cotton produced a 500-pound bale. Picked, about fifteen hundred pounds would "gin-out" a bale.

Pick or pull, the experience rests in the back of one's mind much like serving in the military during wartime. The memories soften with the years and make interesting stories for old men longing for their youth, but few want to go back to it. Still, like the romance of wheat threshing, a memory of those long-ago cotton fields brings some degree of pleasant nostalgia.

Reverend W. D. Hines remembered picking cotton at Bryan in the 1930s. "Oh, I've seen them grown men pull a thousand pounds a day, I never did, but I've seen it. But I never did pull cotton, in my time we picked it. I wasn't much good at it. My wife was. She could pick 350 to 450 pounds, depending on the crop. Me, I'd do good to get 175 pounds." W. D. laughed; it had been a half-century, but he still found humor in his wife beating his effort.

Like the state's settlement, Texas's harvest season starts in the warmer and lower elevations of the south and eastern section of the state then moves westward. In the old days, when gathered by hand, cotton produced on the plains was pulled two or three times during a single season. The first harvest generally started in October with the last gathering (scrapping) performed after frost.

Farmers are often unsure if weather is more friend or foe. What's good for one crop may be bad for another. Country lads decide the matter on simpler terms. Moisture that delays the start of the day's cotton pulling is good. Clouds sending schools of shadows racing across the scorched midday fields, offering momentary relief from a relentless sun, are friendly. At ten years of age on an October morning I relished the late start we owed to heavy dew.

It was 9 A.M. and the sun rapidly burned off the last moisture, leaving the cotton stems brittle enough to snap. A weekday, school had been dismissed for three weeks to make available a labor force of both children and teachers to gather the community's cotton crop. I lifted the broad, heavily stitched shoulder strap of the new ducking sack and placed my right arm and head through its opening. The fresh scent of the processed material mixed with that of cotton leaves and careless weeds, and I felt strong and ready and grown. The morning smacked of freshness, and the waist-high plants stretching across the field had yet to become the enemy. The scent of my Uncle Ray's last drag from a homemade Dukes cigarette drifted across the rows, and he winked at me then shook out his long cotton sack.

Mr. Aiken stood between two rows, next to Ray. A tall man, Mr. Aiken was the principal of Hefner's rural three-room school. My sack measured about seven feet. Ray's was a couple of feet longer, and Mr. Aiken's seemed twice as long. Instead of being boxed-in, or stitched, the end of his sack was tied with a heavy cord. Strapped to both his legs were leather kneepads. Crawling offered relief from bending. I liked Mr. Aiken. He reminded me of Gary Cooper.

We started those first rows near the wagon. Ray and the schoolmaster each worked between two rows, cleaning four as they moved along. I straddled one and worked to keep up. The strap positioned the sack so it hung on the right side. Its opening flapped there near my hip pocket about where Gary wore his six-gun. I grabbed a boll between the fingers of each hand, jerked them free of the stalk, and bit off the too-tough extra stem from one while reaching for a third.

Mr. Aiken's fingers darted from boll to boll; somehow, the flap on his sack hung open so he never had to waste time fiddling with it. He asked, "Know, yet, what pulling's going for this year, Ray?"

"Guys over at the gin said a penny a pound."

"I'll swear. Beats teaching."

"Yeah, I always wanted to make a penny a minute. Today, I'm gonna do it," Ray said.

They were moving away. I pushed green leaves aside with my right and grabbed for a boll with my left. Searing pain lodged beneath my fingernail. A red splotch formed at the end of my heavy, cloth glove. I jerked off the glove with my teeth then stuck the bleeding finger in my mouth. I removed it, shook the offending digit, then dangled it to one side while the blood dripped. I stifled a cussword then another and groaned. Working in the same field with the school principal had its disadvantages.

A black lady a few feet ahead turned. "That sho do hurt. Don't it?"

"Yes-um."

"I know you. You that Murdock boy."

"Yes-um."

"Wal, I'll say. Your daddy owns a grocery store. What you gonna do with all this money?"

"Don't know, ma'am."

Cotton bolls crack open lengthwise when mature. The four pointed sections of the hull dry, curl backward, and harden into something like the barbs of fishhooks. The cactus-sharp points split cuticles, dig under nails, and after a few days turn the toughest hands into sore and worthless appendages.

I remember mother telling of seeing her father wrap his bleeding hands in strips of cloth and going back to the fields after supper. He and some of the boys would work by moonlight until stopped by the dew.

When pulling cotton, an effort is made to pull far enough up the row and away from the wagon so that the return leg will fill your sack as you near the scales. Most "hands" went to the wagon together. Ladies and girls worked side by side with the men and boys, but the males generally handled the muscling of the sacks at the wagons. Handling these heavy sacks for the ladies was considered proper respect. Adding cotton, hence money, to a receptive lady friend's sack fell more under the heading of flirtation.

Scales hung from an angled board fastened to the wagon's side and extending beyond its tailgate. A short rope hung from the hook at the center of the scales. It was not unusual for an athletic man, like Mr. Aiken, to pack nearly a hundred pounds in his sack for each weighing. Afterwards, considerable strength and energy were required to hoist it to the top of a near-full wagon.

The men would arrive at the scales with the sack, stuffed and packed tight, resting on their shoulders. A deft move would snare and fasten the scale rope to the heaviest part of the sack. Then it only remained to disengage one's arm and head from the strap. With the strap wrapped around the scales hook and the sack hanging free, the pea was adjusted along the numbered and notched blade of the scales until it balanced on the proper weight.

Weighing and emptying was a cooperative effort in spite of side bets and competitive natures. One man would mount the wagon and another "handle" the scales. Another stood by to assist in hoisting the heavier more fully packed sacks skyward, to the man above. Often, a second man would be on top to pack the wagon's load by trampling it. Seeing Mr. Aiken, standing high atop the wagon's load, lift his ninety-pound sack to his shoulder then empty it by pulling the cord answered my question as to the reason for his tie string.

Generally the farmer or a member of his family audited the weighing and recorded it on a tablet affixed to the side of the wagon. As wages were weight dependent, disputes were to be avoided. Given true weights, the only larceny left would be the loading of rocks, green bolls, or leaves in the sack to cause it to weigh heavy. Conditions in a cotton patch are not conducive to arguments staying nonviolent so they were avoided if possible.

Throughout that hot, back-paining day, Ray and Mr. Aiken fought time for their penny-a-minute wages. They seemed to share a common respect. Their adult conversation was free of brag, vanity, or profanity. They spoke of prices, crops, and war and I enjoyed listening while chaffing in shame at my own salty and newly acquired expletives. I was unaware that soon both would wear army khaki and long for the peace and discomfort of that cotton patch. We whistled and worked and fussed at our aches and the heavy sacks. At intervals throughout the day our companions raised their voices, singing their way through the miseries of that cotton patch. The year was 1941.

There are worse places than maize fields in August; Normandy on D-Day, the Frozen Chosin (Korea) in 1950, and probably the Japanese can think of a couple, still, it's as near an abomination of the devil as most can conceive of. First it's hot—hot enough that the earth radiates heat through thick leather shoe soles and iron rimmed wheels raise blisters on bare skin. Chaff stings and burns and drifts on the breeze then filters into every opening in clothing. Collars rub necks raw and eyes burn.

The old-timers worked with and gathered maize by hand. That is, they cut the heads of grain from the stalk with a knife then threw them one handful at a time into a team-drawn wagon. Generally two men worked to each wagon.

With its two-and-a-half-inch, blunt-ended blade, a maize heading knife is not that different from a regular man's pocket knife. It's just a little more bulky. The handles are broad and thick enough to fill a hand for a good grip, and the blade is almost three-fourths of an inch wide. Always made of the best steel, a razor-sharp edge lurks, waiting to reward the man with a good whetstone. This tool and the sweat of its owner served as the combine harvester for the maize crops produced in Texas prior to World War II.

The team involved in the maize harvesting were hitched in typical fashion to the wagon, but upon reaching the maize rows, they operated without a driver. The cutters hollered demands. The sound of either animal's name would move them forward, and "whoa" would stop them. At least that was the way it was supposed to work. They were trained to stay between the rows without drifting.

Doyle Conine knows the good side of draft team nature, and he also knows the other side. "Those mules would work that wagon pretty good without a driver until they got full and the wagon began to get loaded. You see, they were ready to stop and eat after a few feet moving forward early in the day. But, they were smart enough to know that if that wagon ever stopped, it took a lot of work on their part to get it started again. Like I say, ours would work pretty good at first, but you better have someone close enough to grab onto that wagon after you'd been at it awhile.

"We kept one person near enough to jump on the back and climb in and get those reins. And they knew what was coming then. We'd run them out into plowed ground and tire them so they were glad to stop when we hollered 'whoa' next time."

At the end of the row the cutter near the wagon had to be ready to jump aboard, turn the team, and line the wagon for the return trip. Most used sideboards on the wagon that were uneven. The higher side acted as a rebound backstop to the flying heads of maize.

Normally the maize was too green to put in the barn until it dried a few days in the sun. After gathering a load, the maize fork came into play as the heads of grain were shoveled out of the wagon onto hard baked ground into mounds ten inches or so in height and a couple of feet wide. After proper drying it was loaded back on the wagon, hauled to the barn, and forked through an opening into a bin for winter usage. Each process allowed more chaff to dry and shatter. Later, almost worn out from handling, and in the team's feed trough, the old mule happily bobbed his head up and down, tearing with momentum the grain from the maize head.

Mesquite, Texas historians recalled old hay-baling days. "The rolling prairie near Mesquite provided good hay. It was first cut with a sickle mower, then allowed to dry for about two days before being raked. The sulky implement with a seat on top was used to form the grass into rows to await the bull rake. Like the other implements, this rake was pulled by a team of two animals, either horses or mules.

"The next step was for the bull rake to gather large stacks of hay to take to the stationary hay press for baling. The press was driven by a horse, harnessed to a long wooden tongue that moved around the press in circles. (Steam powered stationary presses were later used.) Hay would then be pressed into sections called 'bats.' These were then pressed together to form a bale weighing from fifty-five to sixty pounds.

"It took two men to wire the bales. The tie-wire man sat on the front side of the press and put three wires around the bale. Another man at the end, called the 'wire monkey,' wrapped wires around the bales so that the tie wire could cut and secure them. The crew would then 'buck' the bales on the hay wagon for delivery to the farmer's barn.

"To cut and bale a typical 160-acre hay meadow took about one week, and the men lived in the fields, going home only for weekends. A cook and cook-shack moved with the hay balers, and the open field was their bedroom. For the well-deserved bath it was straight to the nearest tank."

One needs little imagination to understand the appeal home must have held for the men on the haying or threshing crews. Clean sheets, cool well water, and the luxury of a cane-bottom chair were only a few of the rewards they looked forward to. The women and children had tended the stock, worked the fields, and kept the home safe for his return. His joy at the reunion was, no doubt, matched by theirs.

Nova Bair is published in a book of poetry and anthologies. Her father farmed on the North Plains of Texas and enjoyed music. She said, "Father played the violin and his first inkling that I would follow in his steps came when, as a child, I picked up the instrument and, without its being tuned, played a little piece." She later taught at the Musical Conservatory in Amarillo. She titled this poem "My Father's Song":

My father sang a song of the land,
This good earth that God has made.
He tended a man-size plot of it,
Pioneering, unafraid.

He planted orchard, planted seed
He waited while he prayed for rain.
He struggled with the briar and weed
And tilled his vale and hill and plain.

He whistled tunes to his sturdy team,
And sang above his tractor's roar.
He shared his harvest with the world.
Because that is what a farm is for.

And in the evening when work was done
He tuned and played his violin.
He taught his children hymns and tunes,
I recall them now as hearing then.

He took us to the schoolhouse church
And later to a steepled one.
He tended well his corner of the world
Until his work on earth was done.

The Homemakers

No matter if they worked for the largest ranch in the country or owned a few acres of row crop pinched in between the big outfits, the old-timers took pride in their work. Notice was taken of the straightest rows and the cleanest crops. Much admiration has been bestowed on the Westerner's loyalty to, and pride in, the brand for which he rode. That same ethic drove the farm hand, the new man working at the gin or the teamster, the trucker or the clerk in the store. It was a trait of the time.

A meritorious reputation by people that had known you all your life wiped out most human failings. "As long as you got your good name, the rest you can get," was the common code of these uncommon people. I heard one old-timer brag, "I got nothing but my name, and I can't spell that, but folks take it to the bank." This creed started with their ancestors, and they did their best to pass it down.

Pride in work and loyalty was as much a part of the old-timer's being as the breath he breathed, and it applied to both sexes. Wherever life's fortunes carried them, most children raised at that time were instilled with this virtue. Having observed it displayed by both husband and wife of that period, I can only assume the child received equal doses from both parents.

The whiteness of a wash, the stiffness of an ironed shirt, and spotlessly scrubbed floors were sources of pride for every home-maker. A woman's reputation in the kitchen was known far and wide. The feeding of farm hands, thresher crews, and neighbors lending a hand provided opportunities for the cook's reputation to build. Church meetings, school socials, and funerals offered other opportunities for excellent homemaking to be noticed. Few higher compliments could be paid than "she sets a fine table" or "keeps a good house."

Norris Curtis had these thoughts in mind when he waved his arm, indicating a plot of ground of approximately an acre and a half inside the small town of Nevada. "See that, that used to be my mother's garden. We'd pick tomatoes by the tubs-full, peppers, five or six different kinds, everything in the world you'd want to eat.

"Talking about all those different kinds of peppers, she'd say, 'I want something different and spicy every day.'

"You see she canned. Metal cans, she used. Folks here in Nevada had a 'canning club.' They could seal those metal cans,

Childhood home of Norris Curtis in Nevada, Texas.
Noris' mother, Mrs. Curtis, in foreground.

before fruit jars became the thing. We'd put up 100 cans of corn every year. We canned chili, roast, and sausage. She kept it upstairs, and she'd send me up after whatever she needed for the day."

Norris smiled, "But the best was those canned sausages and ribbon cane syrup. A fellow came by every year from down east of here. He raised cane and made his own syrup. He'd put it up in gallon buckets. Daddy would buy several cases. Sometimes it would about half turn to sugar, but Maw'd just heat it in hot water, and it'd go back—good as new."

In 1900 Mrs. Duff Green kept a boardinghouse in Dickens. D. B. Gardner of the Pitchfork Ranch and the "Kid" came for dinner with Col. John A. Green.

"I recall, I had salt 'raisin' bread for hot rolls and how they seemed to enjoy them, the Kid asked me for the recipe, he was then batching at Croton Camp."

Ninety-one years old, Carl Nicholson could not hide the longing when he spoke of his grandmother's cooking. "Grandma was just about the best cook in the world. She made biscuits that were small but plentiful for every meal; and she served them with butter and honey, syrup, preserves or jelly. She made a hot potato salad that was almost as good as ice cream. Fried chicken was the rule rather than the exception and there was always plenty of cream gravy to go on the biscuits. She usually had a cake of some kind and always a plate of cookies. She called the cookies tea cakes and I never knew of

Carl Nicholson

her making any other kind: which was all right with me because they were the best cookies I have ever eaten."

Haskell's historians state, "Work was hard on women. Cooking for many years was done at the kitchen fireplace. Both the kitchen and dining rooms were separate from the other rooms, perhaps to make the other rooms more pleasant, particularly in the summer."

They add, "Nelson Walton, of this community, went to Galveston and brought home, by wagon, a cook stove that had arrived by boat."

They didn't say how long Nelson's journey took by wagon, but the stove had at least 400 miles after leaving Galveston to get its sea legs adjusted before arriving in Haskell.

Another among the many difficult chores of those gallant ladies was washing. The earlier settlers did "laundry on the bank of the creek or a large brook, where the clothes were 'battled' on the rocks." From the scarcity of water in some Texas creeks it's likely that laundry was done intermittently.

The later old-timers dug wells and built cisterns for their water supply. Some women dreamed of having the luxury of close-at-hand water. Even if it wasn't carried, the poor lady had to almost wear it out on wash day by drawing it in a bucket, boiling it in a pot, and then pouring and wringing it through subsequent rinses.

In western areas of the state, where low humidity makes evaporation available to perform cooling, water levels also had to be maintained in the milk pans. These were pans with a depth of approximately four inches and an area of maybe three feet square that were maintained in a secure place with a couple of inches of water. Milk in crock jars, butter, and eggs could be kept in this pan with damp cheesecloth covering the containers and touching the water level. Produce could be kept fresh for several hours in this manner. The lower the humidity the better it worked.

A daughter of a Haskell family, the F. G. Alexanders, recalled pleasant kitchen sounds from turn-of-the-century activities. "Each morning before breakfast, the sounds of coffee being ground, butcher knives being sharpened and scraped across the edge of an iron skillet, and steak being beaten with a hammer filled the kitchen.

"Breakfast consisted of steak and cream gravy, or after hog killing time sausage, hot biscuits, eggs that had been gathered the evening before, and plenty of rich golden butter. Children were not allowed coffee, but sometimes a cup of cambric tea was given them. That was a cup of hot water with milk and sugar. Each member of the family must be on time for the blessing or would take his plate to the floor to eat. It never happened but one time, too disgraceful."

Mrs. E. M. Regen wrote, "When my mother wanted to make light bread or buns, she might wonder aloud who had the yeast. The everlasting yeast was passed around and was the responsibility of each neighborhood bread maker. Before the final flour was added, a ball of dough was dropped into a teacup. It rose and ballooned over the top of the cup and formed a dry, hard crust. That, crumbled into warm water and a small amount of flour, was the starter to make a foam for the next batch."

Not too far from Haskell, across the line in adjoining Knox County, Mrs. John "Dicie" Turner Goode remembers early homemaking, her mother's care, and the role of children participating in early day activity.

Mrs. Goode recalled, "I spent a lot of time on a horse. We herded turkey a-horseback to keep the coyotes away from them and still lost some stolen from the opposite side of the herd. We children also rode fence and stapled loose wire.

"My mother used to dab coal oil around my bedroom at night to keep the mosquitoes away."

Knox County historians record, "Mrs. Goode's family moved into a two-room house on the old Hoblitt ranch. One of the men that lived there earlier tried to hang himself from the ceiling in

Turkeys in the street. Mrs. "Dicie" Goode recalls herding turkeys on a horse.
Photo courtesy Texas State Library and Archives Commission

one of the rooms. 'After experiencing several sandstorms, I thought perhaps his action was excusable. We had much worse sandstorms fifty or sixty years ago.

"'I kept account of the number of rattlesnakes we killed over the thirteen years we lived there; the little book was later destroyed and I've forgotten the number—but it was a lot of snakes.'"

At an early age girls like boys did their share of adult work. As mentioned earlier, females often went to the fields to work alongside men. Frequently, the household duties were turned over almost entirely to young girls. Sisters might find themselves responsible for different duties, for instance one caring for the cleaning while another cooked or watched smaller children.

Meals varied with the economy, which for many old-timers in Texas was governed as much by the weather as any other factor. Most of what was served on the tables was home grown. During years of favorable conditions gardens flourished. At a certain stage, field corn provided roasting ears then later a source of feed for the livestock that produced meat, eggs, and milk.

W. D. Hines thought of early country life. "My mother made butter. Some we used—some we sold. Fifteen to twenty-five cents a pound is what she got for it. We had a dasher churn. Us kid would churn that butter." W. D. went through the motion of raising and lowering the dasher. "I can almost smell that buttermilk," he said.

In the west, wild plums provided jelly, and the orchard behind the chicken house supplied peaches. In the south and east the woods and favorable rains added many forms of grapes, vegetables, nuts, and fruits that were not available in the more arid climates. The earlier Texans found game more dependable, but their children, the old-timers, ate better.

Before and after the Great Depression and its Texas companion, drought, Sunday dinner frequently offered a choice of three different meats. Chickens, hogs, and beef were often butchered where they were grown—at home. At least one strapping young man went off to the Korean War with the nagging uneasiness that his hundred-and-five-pound mom could wring a chicken's neck from its body while he searched for the hatchet.

The most common early mainstay of the Texas diet is remembered by Rex Felker. He credits the Great Depression with popularizing "Texas strawberries," known to modern Texans as "red beans" and to most of the rest of the world as ordinary pinto beans.

He suggests cooking them "in a big pot on an old wood burning range. Cover them well with rain water, season with just the right amount of salt, pitch in a few slabs of fat bacon, called sow belly, add enough chili pepper to make them truly red in color, and let them cook for about four hours."

He reported, "An ample helping of this masterpiece of culinary art, along with a thick slab of homemade corn bread and a slice of onion, makes a meal that will satisfy the most fastidious diner."

To my recollection taste has never been suggested as a negative to Texas strawberries, though others from smaller and more confining states have complained of side effects that prove embarrassing.

According to Mrs. Mamie Sypert Burns in her excellent book *This I Can Leave You*, a puncher on the Pitchfork solved this problem many years ago. He suggested to his sidekick, while mumbling something about having rather deal with the "hee-cups," to "cook them beans upside down."

The Pitchfork is, and for many years has been, one of those giant Texas ranches that long ago recognized the value of setting a good table for its hands and neighbors. The following occurred in the 1960s and documents their reputation. Van Thornton, from nearby (sixty miles) Goree, Texas, contracted with Jake Murdock to haul a truckload of horses. Van had bought and was to pick the cowponies up from the Pitchfork. At that time Van was a widower. Eating out, and one's own cooking, will only go so far.

The two men agreed on the deal and the date, and in keeping with good stock handling custom, Dad asked, "Want me to come by for you before daylight so we'un handle them horses before it heats up?"

"Naw, Jake, wait until about ten, that way we'll catch dinner at their cook shack."

The town of Canyon is farther north than the Pitchfork ranch, and in *The Randall County Story*, the writers of that history fail to be daunted by a menu of red beans. They celebrate their early diets and hold that cooks are nowhere more capable of turning the common into the exquisite than around the Palo Duro Canyon.

"Some ate the prairie dogs. The prairie dog is not a dog, but a squirrel. When he came to the plains and there were no trees, he adapted himself to the environment the same as the pioneer. He went underground and in so doing wore his tail off. The meat of the prairie dog is white, juicy, but very sweet."

Mrs. Taylor of that same source writes, "One day when we were having prairie dog, guests came for dinner. When they left they told me that was the best chicken they had ever eaten. I hope my face did not turn red."

While the menfolk struggled with their maize fields, the homemakers dealt with the devil's other favorite—the hot iron. Common agreement abounds that the household iron ranks high among the inequities added to the female gender's burden. According to the *Canyon News*, Dec. 22, 1966, by Lorena Miller, the art of ironing proved a lifelong fund-raiser for Mrs. Alice Fogarty. Alice said, "I first started ironing for the public in about 1913. I had my own laundry service for a number of years.

"When I started ironing the wages were fifteen cents per hour, and I did about three washings and ironings a day, walking from house to house. The irons were different then. We used an iron heated on a stove and then clipped on the handle. You ironed with it until it got cool and then got another iron."

Not only did these good women keep their men and children clean, fed, and clothed, they also civilized the males and made behaved little ladies of the girls. They kept the Good Book in a place of prominence and the animals outside and off the porch. After generations of obedience, submission, and just plain being taken for granted, the end of the First World War saw change brewing among the fairer sex.

Again, Mrs. Regen, formerly Miss LaVern Cummins of Haskell, offers insight, "Mrs. Morton, who lived on the next street, was interested in women's suffrage several years before it became an amendment to the constitution.

"She believed in starting with the twig, so she started a little club of young girls who came to her home for some twig bending. I went to two or three meetings. She gave me a little leaflet to read. I think it was called 'The Suffragette.'"

We're beaten back in many a fray,
But greater strength we'll borrow.
And when the vanguard rests today
The rest shall rest tomorrow.

In Scandinavia trees were bent into shape for boat keels while they were growing twigs. Mrs. Morton may be the only one to have adapted this practice in treeless West Texas. Meanwhile, back in the woods near Jefferson and extending down through Wood County and on south, the East Texas sawmills and the hardy folks who worked them were busy trying to support a growing state's timber demand.

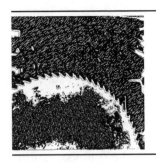

Sawmills and Heavy Loads

As area cultural centers, Canyon and Amarillo are to the old-time Panhandle Texans what Jefferson is to their counterparts in Northeast Texas. With their geography and natural environment more different than many nations, it is natural that the two areas differ. East Texas was settled three-quarters of a century before the Panhandle, making Jefferson relatively old in Texas terms. It grew from a river port, plantation settlement to a town of commerce and a player in the lumber industry. Canyon, on the other hand, had little water and only cow patties to fuel a fire. Still, each is robust and an excellent representative of its area and heritage.

A Texas-flavored sense of Western lore literally drips from the lips of a Panhandle resident when he mentions the T Anchor Ranch, the Palo Duro Canyon, and Charles Goodnight. Meanwhile, over at Jefferson in Marion County, the old-timers drop names like Caddo Lake and Big Cypress, and refer to stern-wheelers of the old days like the *Lizzie Lea* and the *Lessie B* with a touch of an Old-South accent. Timber is close to their hearts.

Sawmills and the lumber industry were revitalized in Marion County around the turn of the twentieth century. Earlier, sawmills were slowed by an expansion of brick construction after disastrous fires during Reconstruction. Later the county's people watched as reduced river traffic, caused by lowered water levels following the downstream breakup of natural logjams, had brought about a decline in population. Now, the treeless Texas Plains were developing and crying for lumber.

In *Jefferson: Riverport to the Southwest*, Dr. Fred Tarpley states, "Jeffersonians again [at the turn of the century] looked with interest at their thick forest. Sawmills, with their accompanying log yards, commissary-supply stores, and workmen's houses were set up to meet the demand for wood products. Business was brisk. Transportation by rail and barge made lumbering inviting once again." Finished product headed west.

For a sawmill family, life was no easier than that of the farmer, but the $2 to $2.50 a day wage usually exceeded what could be wrested from the land. Laborers turned to the sawmill to feed their families.

In Ouida Bailey's article "Marion County Scrapbook," in the Jefferson *Jimplecute*, August 19, 1982, Fred McKenzie recalled his father's mill near Mims Chapel in West Marion County. "There were no wage-hour laws, no workmen's compensation nor social security. If anyone got hurt on the job, it was his hard luck! Some sawmill owners thought it better to lose a worker in an accident than to lose a good mule. Loss of a mule meant shelling out cold cash to replace him.

"Sometimes the mill owner felt obligated to furnish a pine box coffin if a workman was killed, but not always. Sawmilling has always been a hazardous occupation."

In the early 1900s eight-wheeled wagons, pulled by several spans of oxen or mules, inched through East Texas forest hauling heavy loads of timber consisting of from one log to several. These lumbermen seldom had the luxury of accessible waterways to float their logs. Their tools were simple but well cared for. Axes, leverage bars, and two-man crosscut saws converted millions of board feet of lumber from standing forest to mill-ready logs.

Sometimes not much more than a clearing in the woods, the most distinguishing characteristic of a sawmill was the steam-powered crane, the high pile of sawdust, and the

Sawmill blade
Photo courtesy Texas State Library and Archives Commission

Sawmill
Photo courtesy Texas State Library and Archives Commission

multiwheeled log wagons. Whining cables, creaking gears, and the puffing steam engine greeted the new load. Upon easing the team into the mill yard, the scent of sawdust mixed with pine tar hinted at the log's fate.

Can to can't were the hours. Loose fitting overalls, heavy brogan shoes, coarse buttoned-down shirts, and nondescript flapping hats completed the garb. The men fit no physical pattern but in general were straight, agile, lean, and able to perform the most difficult tasks for hours. Missing fingers were common. More severe losses were not unusual. One might pull cotton by moonlight, but wrestling timber around a screaming saw blade that ate logs, cut whatever it touched, and spat planks ended with good light.

At nineteen Frank P. Dannelly worked for the Ware and Driskill Lumber company at Sarber, nine miles west of Jefferson. He became manager of the commissary. Later he wrote and was quoted in Ouida Bailey's article, "If an army marches on its stomach, so does a sawmill work force. It was not uncommon to dispense daily fifty cases of soda water, two 38-pound hoops of cheese, fifty pounds of summer sausage, dozens of fried pies and other pastries, in addition to apples, bananas and other fruits, as well as ice creams."

Throughout the wooded counties of East Texas, from the Red River to Houston, timber challenged cotton for importance. The large mills weren't the only ones competing. Some mills consisted of little more than a truck with its wheels jacked up and attached to a belt running one of the giant blades. A few miles south and west of Marion County, Wood County also put its timber to commercial use. Hundreds of railcar loads of cross ties were shipped. Pine Mills, Perryville, Ogburn, Merrimac, Peach, and Fouke began as sawmill towns and survived as Wood County community sites.

The uses of timber were as varied as the trees in the forest. Pulpwood for paper found an early market, and with the coming of the discovery of oil, heavy timber for derricks became a major product for many mills. Telephone poles and fence rails found a limited market. West of what is considered the forest area of Texas, even the lowly Osage orange, or bois d'arc, found a place for itself as a hedge fence. Texas timber offered an escape from the plow for many workers.

In the Plains areas, cotton gins took the place of sawmills as the hub and industrial center of the community. They also provided seasonal employment away from the farm. The work was long, hard, dirty, and dangerous. Experience came fast. Dad was under twenty when the following incident occurred, still, he was a veteran gin hand. A friend a year or so younger came to work at the gin. Dad loved this pal as only men with great respect for one another can. The two kidded back and forth and had many a good laugh together, usually at the other's expense. When my father saw this guy coming his day brightened.

"I'll never forget the first fall old 'Nail' worked at McNeil's gin, Dad said. You know how stout he is. I bet he weighed 230 pounds even then. Mac had an old truck we moved cottonseed with. Well, this particular day, we'd caught up ginning for a few

Left to right: L. P. McNeil, J. T. Murdock, fourth from left Ferris Mobley, far right Clarence Jones. Hefner (Knox County) gin crew.

minutes, and Mac and a bunch of us were all standing around the scale house. Nail had been working for only a couple of days at that time. One of the guys eased up there with a big load of cottonseed on that old truck and stopped and hung his head out the window.

"'Who's going with me to unload this cottonseed?' he asked.

"McNeil said, 'Nail, Son, get in and go with old Bob and help him unload that truck.'

"Nail looked sort of funny. 'Humph,' he said. 'Get in and go unload 'em yourself if you want 'em unloaded.'" Dad couldn't restrain himself. He bent with the laughter.

"Well, old Mac, he just got in the truck and they drove off. Awhile later, Bob drove the empty truck by and let Mac out. He was sweaty, had his suit coat on his arm, and the vest unbuttoned over that big paunch of his. He looked around and seeing Nail had gone back out to the gin, he shook his head. 'What's wrong with that dern boy?' he asked."

By the time another season rolled by, Nail found his earlier lack of experience amusing, also. When reminded of the story he would laugh. "Heck, I was just a big ole kid, had never worked away from Daddy."

Hearing this story, Doyle Conine's face lit up. "I saw something like that once," he said. "Me and this big old kid hired out to help an old fellow that was a neighbor of ours. The old man said, 'Boys, go over yonder to that garden and dig up them Irish potatoes and we'll sack 'em up fore it gets too hot.'"

"Guess my buddy thought it was already hot enough for he said, 'You want 'em, go dig 'em up yourself, you know where they are. You planted 'em!'"

Dad wasn't always the most experienced one in his group. During the 1960s Joanne and I carried my grandmother, Mrs. Sid (Nettie Brown) Murdock, to Abilene to meet with family. Her home was in Wood County. We drove west through downtown Dallas.

Sid and Nettie Murdock with their first four sons in 1912.
Left to right (boys): Vernor, J.T., Arlin, Cecil.

Grandmother looked at the tall buildings, so familiar to her but always a wonder. "Sid and I and the kids came right down this road in a covered wagon. Let's see, that must have been about 1913. I remember because I was pregnant with Ernie

Mae, and J. T. was little more than a baby. Not big enough to stay up with Vernor and Cecil."

"Where were you going?" I asked.

"Jones County. Ernie was born out there. I told Sid once, every time I got pregnant we moved. Cecil was born in Ward County, Vernor and J. T. in Wood County, Ernie in Jones County, and Wyman in Baylor County."

It seemed time passed swiftly that evening. Grandmother enjoyed Joanne and our two daughters, two of her earlier great-grandchildren. The DFW turnpike was smooth as a runway then, and shortly Fort Worth was in my rearview mirror. We crossed the Brazos and later climbed Ranger Hill. The conversation waned. Darkness surrounded us.

"I guess you slept in the wagon at night." I said.

"What, oh, the trip to West Texas. Yes, we'd just park somewhere there was water beside the road. We lost Cecil and Vernor along here one evening." Grandmother chuckled.

My interest was piqued. I knew Uncle Vernor and Uncle Cecil to be a handful, but I'd always thought Grandmother must surely champion them. "What happened?"

"Well those two were like worms all day long in that wagon. By evening they were ready to roam by the time Sid got the team unhitched. Well, this particular evening we were up on this prairie, flat and treeless. The last I saw of the boys, they had spotted a prairie dog and were running toward him. As I said, J. T. was too small to be with them right then. After a while, we missed them and started calling. I was scared to death."

"Where were they?"

"Sid finally found them. What happened, each time they would get near a prairie dog he'd go down into his hole. Well, by that time another would pop his head up fifty yards or so farther out. They ended up, I don't know how far away, but they were totally lost."

"They were a mess, I bet."

"They were good boys, just mischievous. All my boys were good." She thought a moment. "But, yes they did stir things up a bit. Did I ever tell you of the time they played that kittens were their horses?"

"I don't believe so."

"The old cat had kittens under the barn. As soon as these little ones' eyes opened and they were able to run around good, Vernor and Cecil discovered them. They had great fun pretending these kittens were their riding horses. They tied a string around the kitten's necks and would lead them around, shoot Indians and Yankees and such off of them. I made them promise to be gentle and they were. They loved their horses. This went on a while then one day I looked out the kitchen window and was appalled."

"Uh-huh." I said.

"Out there, hanging by their neck ropes tied to willow limbs, were those two cats, about three feet in the air." Grandmother made a move as though smoothing a nonexistent apron. "They'd decided to tie their horses while they went into the saloon, so they pulled two limbs down to where the cats stood on the ground, tied them, and walked off."

"Were the cats dead?"

"No, I finally got them cut free. I made the boys promise if they wanted to ride horses anymore to get a stick. It didn't matter though, for those two couldn't catch those cats for at least the next month."

"This treeless country must have seemed strange to a young wife from Wood County."

"It did, especially on out in Jones and Ward Counties. This had all been settled for some time by then, but out there a lot of those fences were still shiny wire."

Growing Fences and Stretching Wire

A cowboy mentioned, "if there are fences in Heaven, believe I'll pass." Despite this general feeling across our state, one of the most common necessities during the early days was a means of keeping livestock safe and at home. Sid Murdock found this to be true when he freed his team in a pasture with inadequate fences at a new site in Baylor County.

"It was in the twenties when Poppa moved us from Wood County," Dad said. "He turned the stock out on this old place south of Bomarton, and the next day he couldn't find the horses. The animals strayed and he lost several days of work looking for his team. Only after borrowing a saddle horse from Mr. Thomas was he able to find the animals. They were miles from home and moving farther when he found them."

Barbed wire came into common use near the end of the 1870s as a fencing material and brought many of its early developers tremendous wealth. One of the larger ranches in the state today, the Spade, near Colorado City, was purchased with funds generated by wire manufactured and patented under the Elwood name. Before that time fences were dependent on the resources at hand. In most cases those resources were rare, different, or nonexistent. Texas's fences are as varied as are the people who built them.

It used to be if you studied fences closely, you could get a little insight into the people who owned them. The safest place to do this is from below. Never look down on fences. At the age of five, I saw a girl fall on a barbed-wire fence. Avoid heights around fences. That's why as a kid I studied barbed wire while lying on my back, that and other more pragmatic reasons like wanting to be on the other side and being too small to open gates.

A smart man once announced a lack of interest to be a forerunner to ignorance. The idea being the more interested you are the more you learn. I've not always listened to his kind, but I have learned to allow fences to arouse my curiosity.

Fences were at one time stretched with propped up wagons, braced with dead men, and, on occasion, even cultivated. There are rail, rock, hedge, picket, drift, ribbon, and just your plain old run-of-the-mill wire fences. One early cattleman, Charles Goodnight, had effective fences provided by the bluffs of Palo Duro Canyon. Today, if they really want to get "sissy" about it, some Texans admit to electric fences.

Landon J. "Bedi" Taylor was born in Ennis in 1903. By his first school year his family moved to Lorain, Texas, in Mitchell County. Bedi and his older brother Kirk hunted wolves as boys south of Lorain, and he once said he believed in those early days there were no fences between there and the Rio Grande. This distance to "The Rios," as he called it, is over 200 miles.

Bedi developed an early love of drugstores and all things modern from having too big a helping of the old-time stuff when just a towheaded kid. His father understood how to make money and was a trader, and whatever he bought it was up to Bedi to care for. Since most of this trade stock breathed and wore hair, young Mr. Taylor found himself herding cattle from the back of a mule when just a kid and doing man-size farming and fence building during the slack time.

A few years ago while hunting on his farm, he pointed. "See that fence?"

"Uh-huh." At the moment, being content with the side of the fence we occupied, I chose to change the subject. "How'd you come to own this place?"

"Don't know why, but Daddy bought it. Sent me down to work it. A few years ago, it came back to me." He paused and lit a cigar. "I built that fence."

"When?"

"Must have been around the first war. Me and Kirk built it."

I looked across the three-quarter mile or so of rolling pasture the four-strand fence guarded. "What did you use to stretch her, those old rope and pulley stretchers?"

"Didn't have no stretchers."

My ears pricked up. I sensed I was about to learn something. Visions of fulcrums and levers came to mind but didn't seem to apply. "What did you use?"

"Used the wagon's hub and wheel. Just drop the tongue, maybe, dig out a little hole and bury the end of it, then prop up a rear wheel. See, when you wrap that wire around the hub then tie it to a spoke, you'un wind it up tight as you want by just turning the wheel."

I was right about the learning. I thought of sailors winding a windlass to raise an anchor. Then my mind wandered to dogs marking territorial boundaries as a vision of a wagon with a wheel hoisted came to mind.

From Jack County down through Palo Pinto and into the hill country one doesn't have to look too hard to find evidence of stone or rock fences built by settlers. Many of these good neighbors are of German and Czechoslovakian decent and from the looks of it, brought skills from the old country that they put to good use.

Earlier, rail fences were mentioned in connection with East Texas. Like rock fences, the labor and transportation costs of this method of livestock control was prohibitive except when the raw material was free and abundant.

The southern half of Texas, the brush country, had few trees suitable for rails. In many areas of that country rock or stones were also scarce. A land of mesquite, salt cedars, and blazing sun, like the rest of the state, its people adapted to what was available and used the thin trunks of cedar for picket fences.

With the possible exception of mesquite, the "crab apple" or bois d'arc has more foul language directed its way than any other tree in Texas. A pest because of its vicious thorns, its ability to drain nutrients and moisture from nearby cultivated crops or meadows, and its iron hard texture, it has nevertheless at various times found a niche of usefulness.

Native Americans valued bows made of this yellow Osage wood. Properly seasoned and formed they were serviceable for many years. Extremely hard and heavy, the wood later found its way into many of the immigrant's wagon wheels and boxes.

As one moves west the pine forests fall behind, and the heavy clay or black gumbo, Osage-friendly prairie lands often replace them. Collin County is one of these areas. In their county's history, their writers pay tribute to a unique method of fence building associated with the Osage orange.

"Long before the arrival of the immigrants, Osage, or bois d'arc, trees grew along the streams in Collin County. The settlers used this wood for fence posts, house blocks, pilings for bridges, and other purposes. Settlers from Ohio, Illinois, and other states were familiar with fences in their home states, so, soon after their arrival in Texas, they began planting the seeds of Osage apples where fences were needed. The *Texas Almanac* of 1868 explained how to grow an effective hedge fence from seeds or cuttings.

"After barbed wire came into use, the Osage hedge was regarded as a nuisance, particularly when adjacent to cultivated fields since its roots and shade prevented growth of other plants for perhaps seventy-five feet."

The Osage fence was not the only casualty of manufactured wire. The metal strands opened up the plains to farming and, with the railroads, closed the gate on trail driving forever.

Some of the first barbed-wire fences were called drift fences. Aptly named, their purpose was to keep livestock owned by the large ranches from drifting out of the country due to weather or range conditions. Some of these drift fences ended at a destination, perhaps the bluff of a mesa or canyon, others just ended. Often they were measured in miles and they all had a purpose—turn the brand.

Many years ago I leaned on the top rail of the livestock sale pens of the Colorado City every-Saturday sale. The sun beat down hot on the shoulders of my shirt, and calves bawled in the pens. Inside, the barn's shade and evaporative coolers aided by the almost constant desert breeze of that country cooled the crowd.

A small weathered old-timer, the son of an early-day fence rider, stood beside me. We were neither buying nor selling. Strangers, we smoked, charged our batteries with the sound, sight, and smell of cattle, and fortified ourselves for the different lives we'd lead the following week. A brief return to this token of the similar one we'd known—me briefly, him for decades—acted as the charger.

We exchanged names and I sensed my new friend had things on his mind. He said, "In my late teens, me and a half dozen other cowboys drove 600 steers from here to Denver." He paused. "Nothing much exciting happened."

I nodded. He continued. "Wal, one thing, when we got a little ways this side of Denver we held up one night just south of Pueblo, Colorado. There sure wasn't much to that place then, but that night we left a couple of the boys with the cattle and the rest of us went in and kicked up our heels some. It turned out there was a little ole shanty red-light district just south of the main town."

"Wal, the next morning, by first light, we were moving that herd north and they had that fresh air in their noses and were stepping out. They hadn't more'n got limbered up and we come up on that shantytown and they broke into one of them little ole playful gallops like fresh stock will sometimes do." My companion chuckled. "They weren't stampeding, you understand, just kicking up and having a little fun. Wal, up on those porches they'd go, around them corners and stringing ladies garments on their horns from them clotheslines. First thing you know, one of them gals' white faces would peek out a window and duck back in then another would do the same from a doorway. You know, they ain't nothing ghostlier than a morning-after honky-tonk gal. It was funny."

My acquaintance said he'd lived in the area all his life. "Dad came here when the buffalo bones still covered the country. He hired on with a large cattle outfit, and they put him to seeing after a drift fence. I believe Dad said that fence started between Colorado City and Sweetwater and extended north almost to the Red River. Several men were hired to do nothing but patrol sections of the fence, keep it in good repair, and turn cattle bunched near it back onto home range."

A couple of guys moved the calves from the lot we leaned on. We shared a little quiet together, stomped and ground out a couple more butts into the sand at the base of the fence. He commented, "enjoyed talking to yuh, young fellar," and walked away. In a moment, I realized he left only his story with me. I'd been wrapped in his yarn and forgot his name. I started to holler after him, but about that time he slammed the door to his old pickup and drove away.

East of the fence my anonymous friend talked of, Mr. S. W. Scott arrived in Haskell County July 9, 1884. Scott said, "The only fence in Haskell County, at this time, was the west fence of the M. O. pasture. It ran from the present Throckmorton Road south, about half a mile inside the east county line, some fifteen miles, to connect with the pasture fence of the Monroe Land and

Cattle Company (the W.O.O. outfit). This latter pasture continued south several miles to connect with the Elleslie Ranch of the
Swenson brothers. This pasture ran west some ten or twelve
miles. There were no other fences in the county at this time.
Afterward, the cattlemen made up a pony purse and built a drift
fence between the Swenson pastures to keep the cattle from
drifting to the Gulf of Mexico.

"During the following years I worked with the cow outfits on
the open range, covering the territory from the brakes on the
Wichita in Foard County to Santa Anna Mountain in Coleman
County, and from Routh Creek in Scurry County to Round Timbers in Throckmorton County. At this time I had ten or twelve
horses in my mount, using half of them at a time while the
others rested.

SMS Swenson pasture and fence January 2000.
Stone markings at the top of the knoll read SM2.

"I think I fenced the first whole section that was ever
enclosed by a resident of the county. This was the Shields

Booker section on Paint Creek, which was fenced in 1886. This land was granted to the surgeon who dressed Sam Houston's wounds at the battle of San Jacinto."

A few miles north, Mr. Price Turner settled two different places near Gilliland. "One of the places, now known as the Reed place, lay one-and-a-half miles north of town. Turner was the first to build a fence. He used ribbon wire, flat and twisted with points shaped on either side."

Building a barbed-wire fence is a combination of hard work, wrestling with razor-sharp wire teeth, and art. Most fence build-ers, while in the act of wiping sweat from their brow and blood from their tattered arms, would deny the art part of the equa-tion. Once the job is finished and they stand back and admire their work standing straight, true, and tight, their feeling of accomplishment is not unlike that of paint-smeared artists. If it is really well built and tight, the urge to reach over and pluck a strand of wire just to hear it sing is almost irresistible.

It's hard to fence sitting down, so most cowboys cringe when assigned such duty. Top hands generally avoid having to share in the chore except when major jobs are undertaken. The battle to get the posts in the ground to the proper depth varies in difficulty with the nature of the soil. In sandy loam, slightly moist, it is a pleasure to feel the manual diggers take a full-size bite into the earth. Along the rocky outcroppings of the badlands, progress slows, and a pointed steel rod and a half-hour's work often yields only a spoonful of dust and a sweat-soaked shirt.

Rivers and other natural boundaries often require curves in the fence line and proper bracing to offset the side pressure gen-erated by these turns. To prevent the fence giving to this pressure and leaning, early builders resorted to the use of a "dead man."

To utilize this dead man, a fencer digs a hole large enough to contain whatever corpse he finds handy, generally a large stone. The grave's depth is determined by moisture and soil conditions, but it must be deep enough to get to soil that will remain stable in the wet season. An angling trench or slit is dug wide enough to permit a looped double strand of barbed wire to run from the upper part of the post down to and around the buried rock. When the dead man is properly laid to rest, tension can be applied by placing a stake to act as a lever between the looped strands and twisting. A "stud-hoss" fence results.

In earlier days men on horseback were the greatest threat to a newly strung fence. History records cases where cattlemen and their drovers, the ancestors to the last old-time Texans, spilled blood over this threat to what they considered their right to market. In some parts of the state, it was unlawful to carry wire cutters in saddlebags.

For most of us today, fences whisk by, a formation of posts and wire providing a border to our right-of-way. Perhaps more functional than artistic, they are a strong reminder of a basic tenet of Texas, the right of ownership to private property. They stand against natural enemies of fire, tumbleweeds, blowing sand, floods, and pressure from the animals they contain.

Cedar posts are most susceptible to fire. Tumbleweeds grow or blow into fences then act as sails to catch wind and buffet and stretch wire. Blowing sand forms dunes in the weeds along fence rows, ultimately burying fence and all. Floods wash away posts, and driftwood sometimes takes whole fences downstream.

A vague childhood memory tormented me concerning fences. Something seemed untold. Barbed wire, always a danger coiled or stretched, is forever ready to draw blood. Why did I sense strands of hated wire could be a source of ritualistic pleasure? I asked an older cousin, Johnnie Loree Miller of Seymour, to refresh my memory.

She said, "Oh yes, I remember more than once after frost, at Granny's, we'd all go out after dark and burn fence rows. The ground would be all laid-by, plowed, and there'd be no danger of fire spreading, It seems to me the wind would be blowing to take the fire in the direction the boys wanted it to go. Well, we'd all have these torches of rags soaked with kerosene and we'd look like a legion of soldiers coming in the night to torch the fortress."

"How many of us would there be?" I asked.

"Well, Ray, Lloyd, and Jimmy and then maybe five or six of us grandkids. Those dry tumbleweeds would burst into fire like an explosion and then break free and roll across that plowed ground, just beautiful at night. Much more spectacular than Christmas fireworks."

"Did we take water to prevent the post catching on fire?"

"I imagine. I just remember that sparkling fire against a black starlit night and Uncle Lloyd playing 'Mama Don't Allow No Fiddle Playing 'Round Here' on his guitar while the rest of us laughed and sang with him."

I knew there was something fun about fences. Actually fun is where you find it, and it seems those just before us were good at the search.

More vital than fences, the need for adequate water for both human and livestock presented a never-ending problem. Not only critical, it was universal throughout the state. In the west, water's scarcity and alkalinity presented a problem. In the east and south its overabundance and impurity presented opposite but equal difficulties. The problems in the west were more apparent, those in the east more sinister. Shallow water tables in those areas of heavy rainfall offered opportunities for pollution, and death from typhoid fever ran rampant for decades before science traced its source to polluted wells.

Many Texas homes were built in areas where the families were dependent on dammed up tank water for their and their livestock's, needs. This situation provided a different use for fences—keeping animals out. In this case, all but the larger tanks were fenced.

Fences and ponds, stock tanks, present more of a problem to some than others. A neighbor, many years ago, built a reputation while carving out a stock tank. A tank isn't a real difficult thing to design. You find a natural waterway of adequate volume and between rains you dig a hole and dump the dirt downstream from the imaginary drainage. The dirt behind the hole forms a dam, and once the excavated area fills then additional water is impounded by the dam, and you have your own great lake. When the digging is complete you wait for rain. My neighbor followed the procedure but became confused and piled his dirt upstream.

He waited with a sense of accomplishment for rain. Sure enough, the next spring it fell. He realized his mistake and told the story around town. He became the butt of every joke, but the following year he put it all into the background by fencing his car inside his yard without a gate.

Many homes collected rainwater in cisterns via gutter systems from the rooftop of the family residence. Where possible, deeper wells collected water from underground sources often located farther from the house. Normally the cistern water contained fewer minerals and was especially prized by ladies for hair rinses.

Cisterns served dual service as a cool storage place for kitchen items and a source of household water. Vivian Hess remembered the family cistern in Hunt County during the 1930s. "In the summer our cistern would get mosquito larva, 'wiggle tails,' in it, and we'd have to strain them out through a cloth of some kind."

The Wichita River empties into the Red River. The Brazos drains directly to the Gulf of Mexico. Near Benjamin in Knox County the two share a common proximity. Their watershed joins at what is called the narrows or the divide. This is a dry, stark, and colorful piece of real estate, loved and romanticized by my mother. The ragged terrain and blending earth tones stirred her imagination and offered a break to the richer, but more monotonous level flatland to the south.

County historians wrote of this region, "When the first settlers came to the Gilliland area, water was scarce. The only permanent water supply was to be found at Turner Springs located south of H. T. Cook's present home. The farmers hauled water in barrels; they put shallow boxes in the ground for the cattle to drink from.

"The first tank built on the divide was called the Freeman tank. The settlers hauled water for drinking and other household uses and also for the stock."

Few raised in this country, at the turn of the century, learned to swim. With their rivers and streams raging torrents in the rainy periods and parched and dry in between, they had little opportunity. Still, one family of early settlers in this arid country had a connection with the greatest water disaster of the century and a near miss with another. Mr. H. T. Cook returned to Comanche, Oklahoma, to move his family to a section of land he purchased near the narrows in 1905. In the family's wagon, with other possessions, were the children.

"As they crossed the Red River, one of the children fell from the wagon into the river. It was three-year-old Venta. Her brothers, Delbert and Sherman, jumped in and got her and the trip continued.

"About 1912, Delbert became ill and his father took him by train to Abilene to the doctor. He was operated on for appendicitis. While Mr. Cook was in Abilene, the family got a wire reporting that a nephew was on the ship *Titanic* when it was rammed by icebergs and sank in the North Atlantic Ocean."

Until age seven Doyle Conine lived in Oklahoma. He said, "East of Blue, toward Bocochita, we often forded a river about two feet deep. The water was a good 100 feet wide. I never liked that crossing.

"Later, after moving back to Texas, we'd go back and visit relatives. When I was about eleven or twelve my cousin that lived up there had learned to swim. Nothing would do but that we go to the creek and he teach me to swim. Well there was a place where I could wade in and paddle and the current would take me downstream and then by this flat rock. Beyond the rock the water was over my head.

"My cousin would sit on the rock and grab me as I came by and pull me out. It worked okay a few times, then the next time, I grabbed him and he fell in with me. He just barely had the strength to push me to that rock. When we got out of there I had taken on a lot of water. I mean I had barely made it."

West of Doyle's home in the dry country, wells were dug where possible, but many areas had no retrievable underground water. Methods of finding water under this condition varied from exhausting, backbreaking work to resorting to "water witches" and the application of the divining rod.

Water witches were a cross between shamans of the twentieth century and "snake oil" salesmen. They claimed to have a sixth sense or the ability to find underground or hidden treasure, water, mineral, or almost whatever was in demand at the time. Their approach to finding underground streams of water generally consisted of using a forked tree limb or in some cases a similarly shaped fork of another material.

Held properly, with a limb of the fork in each hand and the single supporting branch pointing skyward, the wonder working would begin. The witch, upon walking over the proper spot, would receive a signal of energetic vibrations emitting from the stick, forcing the point downward and marking the spot for the hole to be dug.

I'm unsure if a witch found the source of water for Great-grandfather Jackson's first well in Knox County, but family legend says in the process of its being either dug or cleaned out, a mule fell in the hole. The well, several feet deep at this time, had no curb. The mule, possibly harnessed to a slip, was more likely providing the lifting power to bring up dirt.

At any rate, a hole in the ground, yards deep, damp, dark, and shared with a thrashing, panicked mule seems a bit cozy. One of my uncles, probably the smallest of the lot, certainly the slowest thinker, tied a rope around his waist and went down and eventually got a loop around the animal's belly, and both were hoisted to safety.

While having coffee with a stranger in Euless, Texas, in 1999, I heard a similar mule story. It had nothing to do with water, but it did have a connection with drinking. I didn't get the man's name, and even if I had, he was from Oklahoma so I pass this story on with reservations.

My coffee-drinking companion said, "Grandfather had large holdings during earlier days and constantly carried a gallon jug of moonshine on a leather tether looped over his shoulder. He also worked mules, and one day when one got down and tangled in his traces, Grandpa tried to help."

Of course the mule, being off his feet, became panicked. "In trying to straighten the mess out, the animal's hoof and leg became trapped between Grandpa's neck and the jug's loop, and Grandpa died trying to save a mule."

Although their mule trouble was common, the outcome was different, and my grandfather was privileged to live and enjoy his good well of water for a number of years. He even managed to equip the well with a windmill to avoid drawing water. Still, it got to the house a bucket at a time.

Prior to electricity, cars, and tractors, the windmill, towering above the flatlands, represented the most complex mechanical apparatus on the farms of West Texas. Those with an aptitude nudging them toward mechanical things found the leather and ball valve assembly that submerged in the water's depth an interesting bit of intrigue. Screeching gears of the dry fan assembly cackled loudly, demanding service. Those with a yearning for flight and high places satisfied the need by climbing the tower.

Nova Bair's childhood trips up her family's windmill near Amarillo had a different purpose. "At noon my job consisted of climbing the windmill tower and tying the tea towel to indicate dinner time to the men in the field."

Windmill on a wooden stand.

As the fledgling aviation age drew ever-larger headlines, the windmill platform proved more and more useful as a staging pad for imaginative minds interested in such things as launching wooden planes, paper gliders, and parachuting horned frogs strapped to handkerchief chutes. The spinning fan announced the rapid approach of the air age.

Religion, Fun, and Social Events

An early Texas requirement for citizenship and property ownership under Mexican rule was a statement swearing political allegiance to Mexico and religious loyalty to the Catholic Church. Protestantism went underground, surfacing only in clandestine home gatherings.

Before the 1900s those of Protestant faith had re-emerged and flourished side-by-side with Catholicism. Still, religious prejudice existed between Protestant denominations as well as between Catholic and Protestant. Fortunately, in most cases, though not all, this prejudice found an outlet in humor and gossip rather than violence.

Widely loved Mrs. Johnny Patton of Goree, Texas, subscribed to the Baptist doctrine. She is quoted as having discussed this with her mother. "We were in the kitchen one day and I said. 'Mother, if you had carried me to Sunday school with you, I probably would have been a Methodist.'

"'How could I take you to Sunday school?' Mother replied. 'I had to stay home and cook dinner for the Baptist preacher.'" Those old enough to remember confirmed that this family truly did board many preachers who stopped in Goree; it made no difference what denomination.

Historians in Haskell County wrote, "During 1887, in what was then known as Rice Springs (later Haskell) W. C. Ballard wrote to a Brother J. W. McGarvey. He asked him to recommend a young preacher who would come for small pay and be willing to put up with many hardships incident to frontier living and existing prejudices.

"Young Brother J. B. Boen arrived in early 1888 and delivered a series of sermons on 'First Principles,' which he delivered with all the power and enthusiasm of an older preacher.

"There was bitter opposition against a 'Campbellite,' as he was termed, preaching in the town, and some of the citizens ordered him to leave by a certain time. They even went so far as to shoot into the room where he usually slept. Fortunately, the young preacher spent the night in another home, thus escaping an assassin's bullet."

Proving that they, like the rest of the state, ultimately became a little better behaved and swapped religious fervor laden with bullets to humor, this same source writes about the practice of faithful members feeding their pastors.

"This particular Methodist preacher thought he would kind of prepare the way for a good dinner, so after Sunday school class let out he stopped Johnny, about ten years of age, and asked him what they were going to have for dinner. To which Johnny immediately replied, 'Goat.'

"'Oh, the preacher said, 'I bet you are kidding. I bet you have fried chicken.'

"'Nope,' Johnny said, 'We're gonna have goat.'

"Sure enough when later seated around Johnny's parents' huge dining table, the boy's mother brought in a big platter of golden fried chicken.

"The preacher looked across at Johnny and said, 'See, I told you we would have fried chicken.'

"Johnny looked up from his plate rather sheepishly and replied, 'Wal, all I know is I heard Pa tell Ma this morning, 'Guess we'll have that old goat for dinner today.'"

Bill Mann grew up near Waco. He was named after a great-grandfather who helped support his family by preaching.

Bill said, "Granddaddy preached in the Methodist church every Sunday for his family's dinner. Back then, that was their salary."

Doyle Conine spent his youthful years on a farm in Hunt County. The mention of earlier religious mores brought a story to his mind that had nothing to do with eating but did shed light on the welcome new preachers received from their flock. Doyle said an old deacon was showing the new preacher around the community. After listening to the history of various families and businesses making up the small town, the young man smiled and said. "You've seen a lot of changes in your time, haven't you Deacon?"

"Yep, and I'uz ag'in every one," came the reply.

Doyle Conine

The Missionary Baptist Church of Jesus Christ was organized on March 9, 1903, in the Mesquite schoolhouse in Haskell County. Its early minutes report, "In keeping with the idea of strict discipline, a committee of three sisters were appointed to investigate rumors concerning the conduct of _____. She was excluded Oct. 10, 1903 for disorderly conduct."

The *Dallas Guide* reports, "In Dallas, still a Western town on February 9, 1883, the only case in the city court was 'a poor specimen of humanity who was fined $1 for uttering an oath.' Standards of morality in Dallas were not what they are today."

Fortunately time and moderation brought tolerance for the beliefs of others, and good-natured acceptance became the norm rather than the exception. Some teased that God intended dry West Texas for Methodists over their immersing Baptist neighbors. The scarcity of water for baptizing was cited as proof.

Week-long brush-arbor revivals capped off with dinner on the ground combined religion with social fellowship. Still, Bibles were well worn and the ox in the ditch was one of the most quoted verses.

Clem Franklin "Doc" Reynolds of early Randell County remembered the seriousness attached to the Sabbath as a rest day. "We drove into Clarendon on Sunday. Mother had to hold up to wash. We had lost track of the day of the week. In the evening, somebody came by and she asked him what day it was.

"He said, 'Sunday.'

"She said, 'Oh, my goodness! I've washed on Sunday.'"

This was the era in which Harris Kempner made his family one of the wealthiest in Texas. Harris lived in Galveston and in reference to the diversity of his Jewish family he stated. "Oh, I've got one child married to a Jew, one child married to a Baptist, one child married to an Episcopalian, and one child married to a Catholic, and I'm president of the Synagogue."

After being cleansed by a good church service, filled to the brim from a heavy laden table, and with the older adults retired to a Sunday afternoon nap, the young looked for entertainment. Baseball frequently filled that need and became a community activity. Played barefooted, often barehanded, and on rough pastureland, it offered an unpredictable semblance to today's game.

Ross Bates remembered a turn-of-the-century game that had to be called rather abruptly. "It was way back there, and in those days we played baseball in pastures or just about any place that had a little flatness to it. This particular Sunday we were playing at a favorite pasture spot near where Bob Lambeth now lives.

"I can't remember which it was, they were both playing with us that Sunday, but either Jim or Luke Jackson got a good hit, and it sailed into the outfield and rolled and rolled then disappeared. Well, when the fielder got to the spot where the ball was last seen he discovered it had rolled into a prairie-dog hole. There was no way to get it out, and since that was our only ball, the game was called off."

A Gilliland, Texas resident wrote, "The ladies organized dances, parties, spelling and quilting bees. Families would fill a basket with lunch, pile into a wagon, and go plum hunting. 'Beef club' members alternated the supplying of a steer for butchering, and the members shared in the day's work. All took a portion of the meat. Literary societies, singings, and revivals added to the list. Men hunted, fished, exchanged work, ran races, wrestled, and held impromptu rodeos."

Rodeo like baseball has been a part of Texas for a long time and has remained relatively unchanged. Today the main difference in both is that now the participants get paid. Earlier the contest served to add excitement to a slow day and create a gathering to kill lonesome.

Mrs. L. S. Jones reminded readers of Haskell County's history that her sons, Grover and Henry, were early participants in rodeo. "The ranch home was at Brushy, in Haskell County, and between them they held three World Champions from the famous rodeo of Calgary, Canada. Each held a championship in bronc riding, and Grover held an additional one for steer roping. They later traveled with the famous Miller Brother's '101 Wild West Show.'"

Fascination with riders of bucking stock always ran deep in my veins, and at mention of rodeo it surfaces. I recently asked Dad about a family story I remembered from childhood. "Dad, did you ever hear the story of Buck (Mother's older brother) saddling and riding a bronc mule backwards?"

"Yeah, I was there. It was a Sunday evening. 'Bobal' and I were dating then, and I was over at the Jackson's. But Buck never got on the mule."

"He didn't. Jimmy must have had it mixed up. He always bragged about what a cowboy Uncle Buck was, and how he rode a mule, saddled backward."

"Buck was a good rider and roper, too, but he never got on that mule. What happened was he told Lloyd (Buck's younger brother) that he'd saddle the mule backward. If Lloyd would ride him then he would." Dad chuckled.

"Course, Lloyd was just a kid, but he watched them ear that ol' mule down and put that rig on him backwards. When they got him steady, Lloyd crawled on."

"How'd he do?"

"Not very good. Aw, he made a jump or two then sailed backward over the mule's head and into the barn. We poured water on him and he came to after a while. By then we'd caught the mule. Buck turned him loose."

About the time Lloyd was being beguiled into his barnyard folly a ninety-year-old Texas lady of German descent passed away. She had arrived earlier with her family at the age of nine. They settled near the Pedernales River west of Austin. Before her death on May 23, 1926, she wrote, "We hurried toward the sinking sun, the magic West beckoning." Thus succinctly stated, Ottilie Fuchs Goeth described the very essence of her memoirs.

She added to our understanding of old-time Texas recreation and social events: "In 1886 a Rifle Club was organized at the Cypress Mill Hall. Apparently it also functioned as the organizational body for the Cypress Mill Club in 1902. Beside target shooting in competition with other clubs there were many other festivities. The food might include about one hundred pounds of beef, goat, or lamb prepared by the men. Then there was bowling, plays were staged, and there were games and contests for the children. And the main event—the big ball at the end of every gathering. Favorite special celebrations were the October Fest, Easter, New Year's Eve, and masked balls."

The *WPA Dallas Guide and History* records, "In 1896 a six-hole golf course was laid out at Haskell Avenue and Keating Street in Oaklawn. It is reported that some citizens were introduced to the game while visiting England. One of these men, Mr. H. L. Edwards, in 1906 helped to organize, and was the first president of, the Texas Golf Association."

The above mentioned source gives evidence that the current rivalry between Dallas and Fort Worth had its beginning long before the turn of the twentieth century. It indicates at that time there were older and more questionable forms of entertainment than golf. Supposedly at one time Dallas was so eaten up with crime and vice that a county attorney considered riding all gamblers and soiled doves out of town on a rail. Learning that Fort Worth was offering them free room and board to come over and stimulate business, a group of Dallas businessmen dissuaded the official from taking his job too seriously. At that point Dallas kept its citizens of questionable repute and Fort Worth had to solicit its own.

They did, however, according to the *Dallas News*, play the first major football game at Oak Cliff Park in 1891. This was rugby football, borrowed from England. Dallas won 24 to 11. "Two years later on Thanksgiving Day, playing the newer American version of football before a crowd of 1,000, the University of Texas triumphed over a Dallas aggregation by a score of 18 to 16. By New Year's Day following, Dallas's players defeated Galveston 20 to 15 at Fair Park where an estimated 2,500 persons saw the scrimmage. Top hats and Prince Albert coats identified the referees in these early games, and despite the roughness of the sport they managed to survive."

It is interesting that, though man had been yearning to fly since the dawn of history, both golf and football came to Dallas before the first airplane arrived in Marfa. C. P. (Cal) Rogers, the "Birdman," landed his airplane the *Vin Fizz* just beyond the stock pens on a field marked by a white sheet. The date was Saturday, October 25, 1911. The local paper claimed everyone in Marfa turned out to see the event.

The flight was an effort by Cal to be the first to fly from coast to coast in thirty days and thereby qualify for the $50,000 being offered by William Randolph Hearst. After a flight of forty-nine days and fifteen crashes en route, Rogers completed his journey. The *Vin Fizz* had endured having most of its parts replaced along the way and earned a spot in the Smithsonian Institution. The plane sported skids attached in front of the wheels and appeared more like a Chinese box kite than something to be flown across the country.

Marfa's location near the southern mountain pass of El Paso probably had more to do with the Birdman's stopover there than their reputation as the "Illuminated City." Still, despite their isolation the area did not lack for an opera house and theatrical productions of remarkable quality. Gilmore Brown was featured in productions there and later operated the renowned Pasadena Playhouse that catapulted many stars into the movies.

One of the largest crowds recorded in the city by 1911 occurred on July 4. This celebration of independence consisted of patriotic exercises at the Opera House, ball games, a barbecue dinner, calf branding, bronc riding, auto races, and a fat man's race.

It would be ticklish to predict which came first in Texas, a running fat man or a horserace, but Dallas could well be the spot it occurred. The *WPA Dallas Guide* verifies that quarter horses ran before the formal organization in 1869 of the Dallas Jockey Club. In addition to horses like Shiloh and Steel Shaft of short track fame, around the 1900s great pacers began to run in Dallas.

"Perhaps the most famous horse ever to appear in Dallas was Dan Patch. In 1904, after breaking the world pacing record in Memphis the previous October by covering a mile in 1:56-1/4, Dan Patch set a track record here by completing the course in 2:01-1/5."

As the years approached the third decade of the century, big changes arrived in entertainment for those near the larger cities. Mesquite historians wrote, "On several occasions in the 1920s, various local merchants sponsored 'Mesquite Night' at the Majestic Theatre in Dallas. Both it and the Palace were multimillion-dollar entertainment centers. The theatres offered silent-film programs and first-class vaudeville stage shows. Then in 1927 the death knell for vaudeville sounded when 'talkies' hit the screen."

W. D. Hines found the circus exciting when he was a boy in Bryan. "We saved up so we'd have enough to go to the circus. In the fall of the year it always came there and stayed a few days. Ringland Brothers, it was."

Mrs. Nova Schubert Bair taught music for many years at the Musical Arts Conservatory in Amarillo. She championed all forms of art and did all within her power to see that culture in the high, north plains country of the Texas Panhandle stayed abreast of that exhibited under the fanciest chandeliers of New England and Europe.

Mrs. Nova Schubert Bair

A student and teacher of both music and poetry, Mrs. Bair is proud of the professional lineage of her instructors, tracing back to the direct teaching of Beethoven. "Beethoven broke with tradition," she said. "He frequently repeated bits of his music as many as three times. Others limited themselves to a maximum of two reiterations. His markings are obvious to me when I see his work." It seems a safe bet the trait lives with her students.

Strengthened with religious convictions, enriched with a zest for humor and fun, and drawing sustenance from the very earth they trod and the waters they sailed, these old-time Texans maintained a sharp eye for nature's signals. Their livelihood, their homes, their existence depended on reaping nature's harmony and dodging or modifying her excesses.

Sensitive to any change and alert for a sign, they watched the moon and skies for signals. Planting was often as dependent upon the phase of the moon as it was moisture. The heaviness of an animal's hair or coat might indicate the severity of an impending winter. Livestock's actions were watched closely and were believed to forecast weather changes.

They prayed for better times and plowed dry earth in preparation for hoped-for rain. Cellars were dug for protection from storms. Lightning rods adorned many houses to guard against bolts from the sky. Along coastlines and on low-lying land, houses were built on stilts. Still, against nature, man is frail, communications are slow, and sometimes warnings are too late or go unheeded.

Nature's Tantrums

Many early Europeans waded ashore in Texas then huddled as seafarers along its shores. With sustenance and safety dependent upon an ability to navigate and understand the sea, those who lived on the coast learned to assimilate folk warnings. Signs of weather changes were among the most closely watched.

In his history of Galveston, David G. McComb preserves some of these old folk sayings. "Mackerel skies and mare's tails make lofty ships lower her sails. Red sun in the morning, sailors take warning. Red sun at night, sailors delight." Others were a halo around the moon and high circling gulls. Once the coastline's coves and bays were charted, Galveston Island became a major port. Her residents bid greetings to many new arrivals.

Sensitive to their own beliefs, the early Galveston founders, like many other Texans, were more callous to the Native Americans' advice. The Indians warned against building Galveston Island into a permanent settlement. For generations they had watched the tempest and suffered its wrath. The city's history states, "In 1810 many Indians drowned while taking refuge on a shell ridge midway down the island."

After a monster tornado, another town in Texas, Wichita Falls, published accounts of the first immigrant residents of the town being told, by the tribes of that region, not to build because of the "big winds." Today's tools continue to prove more of these early warnings valid. Recent video camera film documented images of Jarrell, Texas's 1998 category-five, multiple-vortex tornadoes creating stick figures of people appearing to walk.

The funnels' antics on film leave little doubt as to the source of the Native Americans' warning. "You see dead man walking, you die."

Mr. Norris Curtis was born at Nevada, Texas, in 1915. He later became a farmer and believed in blooming where he was planted. In 1999 I interviewed him on the site of his birth.

He talked of bad weather. "The worst we ever had was the tornado of 1927. We were living right here and it came up, May 9 at 3 A.M. We kids were asleep. They talked about waking us up and Ma said, 'Let 'em go on a-sleeping.' It didn't do much damage to our house, but it wiped out the southwest part of town, killed seventeen people. They made a morgue out of the Baptist Church."

First Baptist Church of Nevada.
Used as a morgue during the aftermath of the 1927
tornado that killed 17 residents of Nevada.

Modern technology mixed with tragedy has taught us the wisdom of those warnings. Tragedy alone held class on Galveston Island on September 8, 1900. David McComb wrote, "At midnight Sept 7th. The moon was bright and there was little sign. The swells were, however, breaking a little longer and with an ominous roar. The tide rose above normal. By dawn it was up two more feet."

For several days, perhaps longer, the worst natural disaster to ever befall the United States had gestated in the warm womb of the Atlantic. It first appeared south of Puerto Rico. Then it snaked through the Windward Islands before moving north-ward over Cuba. It slowly reached the western side of Florida.

"There it returned to sea, gathered strength, and moved parallel to the shoreline of Louisiana then Texas until it arrived south of Galveston. In the afternoon of the eighth, it turned northward, and the eye passed just west of the Island."

The number of people in its path is debated. The number of human bodies in its wake could only be estimated. "The best guess settled at about 6,000 in Galveston alone. Joseph Cline, brother of chief climatologist Isaac M. Cline, sent a message by phone to Houston that Galveston was 'going under.' The whole town became awash."

Many houses were built on stilts, and of these many of the stronger ones, though standing in breakers, might have survived except for the ravages wrought by uprooted trolley tracks and debris that thrashed in the surf, slashing and cutting through the strongest pilings. The reaper of death would not be denied.

The next morning hurricane flags—two red squares with black squares in the center—flew in tandem above the sightless eyes of corpses awash in the saltwater and debris of what had been the town of Galveston. Dazed survivors floated to safety or clung desperately to swaying buildings. In at least one saloon the customers rose from second floor rooms and looked with bleary eyes over the death and destruction that had been their town only the day before. Forced by early rising water to climb onto the bar, they had later retreated up the stairs and slept through the night's raging storm.

A few days later, with cleanup underway and bodies being burned and disposed of in as civilized and rapid a manner as possible, a visiting associate of the editor to the *Galveston Daily News* suggested the Galveston paper man move his operation inland and continue production from there. McComb reports, "With tears in his eyes and a curse on his tongue, the editor shook his fist at the man and exclaimed, 'This is our home. You don't understand how it is. We'll stay and it will be rebuilt.'"

Some did move away, others stayed, and newcomers joined in the rebuilding. Galveston, originally the hunting grounds of cannibals, later home to Texas's most noted pirate (Jean Laffite), and the future gem of Texas gambling and prohibition speakeasies, rose from the brine of the bay. Today, with an indomitable spirit, courage, and a new seawall, this port on the Gulf continues as interminable as the waves that lap her shore. With the aid of a red sun at night, it continues to add a special tang to the Texas flavor.

Freshwater floods routinely mimicked the havoc wreaked by saltwater on Galveston. Along the streams and rivers of East Texas and the Hill Country to the west, thunderstorms and their accompanying floodwaters were a constant threat to the old-time Texans. Less frequent but no less deadly were the flash floods of the flat and dry lands of the West.

Historians in Knox County remember the flood of Friday 13, 1930. "It was the worst flood ever known in this part of Texas, sweeping over parts of Throckmorton, Haskell, and Knox Counties, leaving five dead and devastation in its path.

"The entire Tidwell family: Oscar, Mrs. Oscar Tidwell, Etna Belle, Oscar D., and Mrs. Tidwell's mother, Mrs. Gilliland perished in the floodwaters of Miller Creek when their house was washed away and torn to pieces by the force of the raging torrent."

This is relatively flat and rolling country. Witnesses reported that the whole countryside was flooded with only raised railroad beds showing. The victims were recovered then later transported along these manmade dikes.

Tornadoes often hold hands with hurricanes and thunderstorms. Either of the three is bad enough. Death and destruction follows in the wake of all. The old-time Texans, like their counterparts in Kansas and Oklahoma, took means to escape the twisters.

Nearly every country home in the upper and western part of the state had a cellar. Neighborhood yards in the towns and cities were also marked by the telltale mound and sloped sheet-iron door that betrayed the presence of these shelters. They were cool places, below ground, and were used for storage of home-canned fruits and jellies. However, their main purpose was to avoid the swirling death that stalked the prairie.

1924—cellar door and mound

These people, ancestors to modern Texans, had no safety nets and nothing to turn to, except their own strength and wits. Ambulances, 911, and community shelters were years away.

From above ground there was little to see of those old cellars. Inside there was even less, still, down in them, there was a lot to watch for—snakes, spiders, bugs. Most were a mere hole dug in the ground with a roof of supporting logs or beams with tin (sheet iron) laid over that. Dirt was piled high and mounded for drainage. An air hole, generally a piece of stovepipe, was placed near the rear and extended upward above the mound of dirt.

A sloping trench with dirt steps provided entrance on the other end. Above the steps was the door that sloped from the mounded dirt at the top of the cellar down to the first and most shallow step. Just above the deepest step was a cross-member post or beam, the favorite place for snakes hiding from the sun. Shelves lined one wall and a bed with an iron bedstead occupied most of the floor space.

Crouched down listening to the thunder roll, watching the kerosene lamp's flame flicker and smoke, many a child paused to consider better behavior. Meanwhile one of the men held tightly to the rope attached to the inside of a heaving door that banged with every gust of wind. Still, a degree of pride rose from those musty old holes. It evidenced caring, planning parents, and grandparents who knew where they were going to be tomorrow.

Hurricanes, floods, and tornadoes represent nature's wrath. More common in West Texas is nature's indifference. On occasion, time stands still, and weather becomes emotionless, asleep, and it forgets to rain.

Mrs. Charles Gordon Cummings, an early resident of Randell County, said, "But life was not always easy. There was the perfect drought when it was so dry, cotton seeds could be found in the soil a year after they were planted."

Cotton is a dry land crop requiring little water. The point is, a breath of moisture is all that's required for a seed to germinate. That one taste of moisture will allow life to begin, then if it gets no more, the embryo plant dries and returns to the dust. With adequate moisture the infant plant breaks through the ground and grows. Mrs. Cummings described a year in which there was not a breath of moisture—the perfect drought.

The second year of the twentieth century did nothing to temper the state's reputation for drought. Knox County historians recorded it one of the driest years. "The cattlemen used

Winchester saddle guns to kill the remnant of mustang horses that spring. There was just not enough grass for them and the ranchers' cattle and horses."

During these dry spells the sun is always there, sapping life-giving moisture from earth and plant and the humans who tend them. The winds lose humidity, and leaves curl, wilt, and turn brown. Dust devils dance and cattle bloody their gums and noses chewing on prickly pear.

Carl Nicholson's family moved to Live Oak County in 1914. "There was plenty of rain the first year we were on the Dolan Place, but the next year was the beginning of a three-year drought for that part of the country. Rain that had been stored in an underground cistern was all used before midsummer, and Dad had to haul water from Jim Johnson's well. We had a well and windmill to pump water from, but the water contained so much mineral we could not drink it; and besides, the wind failed to blow very much that summer so we were short of bad water and had no good water at all.

Bladeless windmill.

"Finally, Dad bought a one-cylinder gasoline engine with which to do the well pumping. But solving the drinking and house water problem did not bring drought troubles to an end. By late summer when there would normally be some grass for the cows and horses, there was only the bare earth. Leaves had been eaten from the trees as high as the stock could reach. The mesquite trees failed to produce their usual crop of beans—a nourishing stock food.

"All the ranchers in the drought area were forced to sell their stock or resort to an operation known as 'burning pear.' There is a great quantity of flat-leaf cacti, or prickly pear, growing on most South Texas ranches. With a blowtorch-type contraption it is possible to burn the thorns off the cacti so it can be eaten. Prickly pear is not considered ideal stock food, but it will keep them alive."

Carl added, "That country can, indeed, be hard. Dad always said, 'It's where only the fittest survive, and they're stunted.'"

Prickly pear cacti available for burning.

Throw your chips in a game west of Fort Worth and every hand will draw drought as a wild card. If you live on the lower side of the States between the Brazos and the Pacific and want green after July, you have to climb a mountain or find one of those beautiful windows in time when the desert blooms from infrequent cloudbursts.

I never had the opportunity to know Mrs. Cummings, but her prior quotes and those that follow lock her in as an admirable selection as one of those old-time Texans of courage, humor, and gumption. She is reputed to have often told the story about the time she went with her husband to market with surplus eggs carefully packed in cottonseed.

"Charles placed the eggs in front of the General Merchandise store in Canyon. While he went on a business errand and I shopped, a cow with a taste for cottonseed marketed the eggs."

Later she adds, "Then came the severe cold spell, when snow covered the ground for two months. It seemed during this time, that my husband was away serving on the federal grand jury in Amarillo, and I was alone at the ranch."

Bedi Taylor told of tending chores when only a boy one winter in Mitchell County. "It was cold when I woke up and it got colder all day. We had stock in a pasture a few miles down the road, and before noon I saddled my mule and headed their way. We had a stack of bundle feed. It wouldn't take long to go down there and throw a few bundles over the fence.

"Soon as I mounted Barney, I started shivering. A saddle horn doesn't turn much wind, and the back of that mule was the coldest place I'd ever been. When I got to the feed, I'd throw a bundle then hide from the wind behind that stack for a couple of minutes then do it over. I made it back home in a few hours and Barney stopped in the front yard. When I tried to get off nothing happened. I couldn't move. I was frozen stiff as stove wood. A little later, Mama looked out the window then came and pulled me down."

Bedi's storm was likely the same one remembered by the citizens of Dickens County as the blizzard of 1918. "Cattle, hogs, and chickens died by the hundreds. It came up early in the morning and lasted all day and night.

"A little boy about nine years old left school and got lost; he came to a big barn and went in. The barn at one time served as a livery stable. Word spread that a child was lost. Men searched the town. Mr. Street, owner of the barn, went to tend his stock and found the child with his cows, almost frozen. The boy's name was Bert McAteer."

Like the floods, the winds, and the drought, hail meant instant economic disaster. Varying from pea-size to as big as softballs, it can wipe out an entire year's work in only minutes. Unfortunately, it does so frequently in Texas. In the most severe storms animals and people caught unprotected in the open face life-threatening risk.

Cowboys caught in a hailstorm were quick to remove saddles from the backs of their horses, taking what shelter it offered as their own. Outdoor workers crouched under tractors or whatever machines were handy. When dark storm clouds rose containing a greenish cast and blowing cool air through summer's heat, the old-timers headed for shelter.

Knox County's historians report, "In 1916 the worst hail ever remembered crossed the divide north and south, about the J. R. Spivey place, then on to the river south killing all the birds and rabbits. Bruises caused by the hail blinded cattle for several days. Most of the cedars were killed."

Northwest of Spur, in the spring of 1924, one of the greatest hail and windstorms ever to visit Dickens County formed. "It covered an area 40 miles in length and from 10 to 20 miles wide.

"Before reaching Spur, the clouds separated, one shifted to the northeast and the other passed to the southwest. No one could realize the danger lurking in the two clouds.

"The cloud passing to the northeast soon brought destruction to everything in its path. Hailstones of enormous size fell, killed livestock, and tore gaping holes in roofs. It lay waste to the young cotton and feed crops that were just up."

The "Dickens Item" column of the *Texas Spur* newspaper that is housed in the Southwest Collection of the Texas Technological (University) states, "The most deplorable tragedy of this storm was the death of little Margie Kerley, the daughter of Mr. and Mrs. J. A. Kerley of the Red Hill Community. Margie and two of her sisters and four of the Jones children and Bertha May Young were on their way home from school when the storm swept down on them in all its fury, resulting in the death of the little girl and seriously injuring the others."

Storms offered danger other than wind, rain, and hail. Cowboys riding high on a horse and farmers sitting on a tractor or plow with metal sweeps in the ground were especially vulnerable to lightning. Often the highest point for miles and with metal horseshoes or plow points offering excellent ground, these men were tempting targets.

Nova Bair's father moved his family from Amarillo to Burkburnett to work his teams in the oilfields. Nova remembered an incident with lightning that happened there when she was only a child. "I was swinging in the yard one day and noticed this cloud coming our way. Not far from the house and on a hill were these huge oil storage tanks with flumes on top. Well, that cloud came on over and all of a sudden lightning struck one of those big tanks, and a sea of burning oil came roaring down the hill toward nearby houses. Father took a team and helped the families save some of their belongings."

Early homes were equipped with grounded lightning rods in an effort to drain off the deadly charges without damage to the buildings. These conductive metal rods were given both functional and ornamental shapes and attached to the higher points of roofs and gables. Running along the eves, they ultimately led to the ground.

The risk of being a casualty of lightning was real, but the event was unlikely. Not so rare were the resulting forest and prairie fires that accompanied electrical storms. Still, even a bigger threat of fire came from manmade sources. After the turn of the century and with the coming of cast-iron stoves, every home had a flue of thin metal running through attics. Often many forms of combustible material were in contact with these stovepipes.

When one considers that night reading, ironing, cooking, heating, washing, and soap making all required open fires, it is little wonder that homes burned and accidents occurred. Tragically, children's clothing was most vulnerable.

In Knox County the H. T. Cook's house burned three different times. Others to lose homes were the Cures, the Groves, the McGuires, and the Browns. The third Gilliland school building was destroyed by fire.

The most disastrous fire in the early 1900s in Dickens County occurred in 1909 on the Matador Ranch east of Afton. The fire started in the shinnery and burned for ten days, destroying several thousand acres of grass and many cattle as well as game. Rumors said nesters who did not like the Matadors started the fire.

Earlier, in August 1890, two prospectors let a campfire get out of control on the Spur range. A bad burn of twelve sections resulted, and the ranch's cowboys threatened to hang the two frightened prospectors from Weatherford but later let them go.

In the mid-1990s the county judge of Palo Pinto County smiled as he reported their county was one of the few in Texas to have escaped loss of county records to fire or storm. Tragedy is no respecter of politics.

Like the weather, the seasons of life press forward. Misfortunes blend with time, courage grows into faith and character, then memories turn to the spring of youth when adventure and amazing zest move all generations toward the next.

Romance Blooms

Ask their women: men don't like displaying their emotions. And the further back in time they lived, the more trouble they had. Thankfully, for future generations, men have, perhaps with gentle coaxing, usually found a means of communicating even the deepest of these yearnings.

Levi Anderson Spain drove a shiny new buggy from Indian Creek to Clear Creek, in Brown County. A highly spirited young mare drew the buggy. Mr. Spain's mission was to court Miss Lizzie Owen. In the early part of 1905, he mentioned, "I think I'll have this mare gentle enough for a lady to handle by fall. Do you want the job?"

Miss Lizzie said, "I'd like to have the job, but would you come to Clear Creek twice a week instead of once, so we can become better acquainted?"

According to their daughter, Mrs. Josephine Spain McHan, they were married at Bangs, in the buggy, in front of the Methodist parsonage, September 27, 1905.

Mr. Spain, though perhaps a little hesitant, adds weight to the point that a decade makes a difference in man's progress toward expressing affection. When compared to ten years earlier he was downright gabby. At least, Dr. Cummins' earlier situation would support that belief.

LaVern Cummins said, "In 1895 young Dr. Cummins arrived in Sparta in northwest Bell County. Soon afterwards the doctor met a pretty young girl by the name of Lena Maude Davis. When the country doctor met Miss Davis it was 'love at first sight.'

"To prove this old story's point, George Cole used to relate that it was the custom then to set the dinner table with the plates turned upside down over the knives and forks until after the blessing was said.

"Dr. Cummins was so preoccupied with the pretty girl on his right that he forgot and spooned his turnip greens to the back of his plate."

There is no mention of the blessing's content or, in fact, if there was one, but thinking of the situation I am reminded of a cowboy grace quoted by John J. Lomax in an address before a folklore society in San Marcos, Texas.

"Eat the meat and leave the skin;
Turn up your plate and let's begin."

Fashions were different and parents sometimes more strict, but life was not all work according to Mrs. John (Dicie) Turner Goode. "We had no automobiles or picture shows but went to parties, fish fries, and dances. There were no beauty parlors, no lipstick or rouge. I saw my first face cream after I married, but I always put buttermilk on my face at night for bleach and used prepared chalk for face powder—we wanted to be really white."

World War II marked the end of the fair skin craze, and suddenly suntans were no longer taboo for the ladies. Prior to that period cardboard from shoeboxes found a secondhand use in the slits of homemade bonnets. Granny still fussed, but the young put on shorts and headed outdoors.

Lora Haskin (Wisdom) Murdock and her sister Flora opened the first commercial beauty shops in Bomarton and Goree, near where Mrs. Goode was raised. Recently, at ninety years of age, Lora did not remember Mrs. Goode as a customer but did recall the times when a visit to the beauty parlor was less a refreshing experience than an ordeal of torture and endurance.

Lora said, "Mrs. Jones, a new customer, had decided to give life a whirl and have a permanent. She had turkeys, and with holidays coming up, I needed a turkey. We made a trade, a permanent for a turkey.

"At that time sister and I opened the shop in Bomarton a few days each week and spent the rest of the time in the shop in Goree. We had the new permanent wave machine in the Goree shop. It was a big thing, electric wires and rods everywhere, and hot! Oh, my goodness! You see, it had these big cylinders, and we wired these poor ladies up and covered their hair with those cylinders and baked that permanent about ten or twelve minutes." Laura tried unsuccessfully to suppress a giggle.

"Well, when this lady came in, I sat her down and she had thin hair. I parted it in little one-inch squares and twisted and curled. I made her some little finger waves and was just about ready to turn that machine on and bake her when she looked in the mirror. I never saw such an expression in my life."

Lora laughed and reached for a tissue. "Excuse me." She gathered breath. "That poor lady was looking in that mirror at all those dozens of little corkscrews, and I guess she thought she was going to look that way forever. I thought she was going to faint. I could just see my turkey flying out that window."

"Did you get the turkey?" I asked.

"Yes, I got her calmed down, told her how pretty it was going to be, and we finished the job, but she didn't stay long after we finished."

Seventy years had elapsed since Mrs. Jones's first permanent, but it was obvious Lora still relished the scene in her mind and savored memories of the unique scent of her beauty parlor. "It wasn't long after that Sister suggested we move the shop to Seymour."

"How'd that go?" I asked.

"Well it started sort of rough. There was already a beauty parlor in the Seymour Hotel. Course the hotel is gone now, but then it was a busy place. Well we opened our little shop and about the second day someone knocked on the door instead of coming in. I went to the door and there stood a woman.

"She said, 'I run that other shop, and they call me the Hell-Cat of Seymour. If you open up here, I'll run you out of this town.' Well, I didn't know what to do. I'd never been talked to like that."

"Who remained in business longest?" I asked.

"I don't remember what became of that lady," Lora said with a flicker of amusement in her eye.

The first quarter of the twentieth century was a time of interesting fashions, mores, and inhibitions. It was also a time of rigid adherence to certain superstitions.

Maggie and Roy Barker were married March 16, 1918, and Crawford and Nora Hipp were married on July 3, 1919. Both men were World War I veterans, and the four young people were friends.

Brother W. N. Jarrett of Emory married both couples. Can you imagine their perplexity and apprehension when Brother Jarrett insisted that they stand with their feet in the direction of the flooring's boards to insure that they would not become "cross-wise" in their respective marriages?

Eustace Kirkendoll lived in Taylor County and described proper behavior between young couples during earlier days. "When a boy asked a girl for a date, she had to ask permission of her father before accepting. In marriage, the boy proposed, then he had to ask the father. If the father refused and the girl was of age, they usually ran away and married anyway."

Here, Eustace briefly touched on a facet of romance and courtship that occurred frequently in the early days of this century. This was the waning days of chivalry. Men protected the flower of womanhood zealously, especially in their daughters, and for some fathers, almost no man was worthy of the daughter's hand. More than one bridegroom found, upon his arrival, the atmosphere around the home of his chosen one laden with anger and resentment. Compounding this problem for the young suitor was the fact that many families were not only headed by a father, but contained stalwart brothers.

Doyle Conine mentioned the practice his grandmother and aunt had of hiding the aunt's suitor in a closet when the girl's father arrived unexpectedly on the scene. Asked if his grandfather disliked the boy, Doyle replied. "Granddad didn't like any man that wanted to court his daughters."

Doyle continued, "When Dad and Mother got married they had to slip off and catch a train to go find a preacher. Granddad discovered the plan and followed. He stopped the train and boarded it hunting for them. Dad hid in the bathroom and Mother covered her face with a newspaper and pretended sleep. He failed to find them and they were married that night."

Lessie "Granny" Jackson was married at age sixteen. She said, "Jim and I had to run off to get married. The preacher married us while we sat in a buggy on the Knox and Baylor County line."

Granny and her father did not reconcile for three years after her marriage. Happily, the rift between them healed after the birth of her third child, my mother. Perhaps it was in my grandfather Jim Jackson's genes to elope with his bride. His father, Andrew, had earlier chosen a bride twelve years older than himself. Still, their wedding involved an escape from Collin County on fast horses, not far in front of Great-great-grandfather Seabourn.

Mary Lois (Banks) Pruitt shed more light on one of these tense events. "When Henry approached my dad to ask for my hand in marriage, he was informed that he could marry Kate but definitely not Lois. This caused some panic, but Dad relented and we set our wedding for September 29, 1907."

Mary Lindley added. "Many of the young people were chaperoned. We were not. When children are raised right it is not necessary. A few girls flirted, but not very many. I never cared for a lot of different boys. My sister Lidia and I had our fellows, and we didn't switch around. We married them, too.

"Weddings were usually held at home but sometimes at the church, though they were not called church weddings. No elaborate plans were made. Friends who had gathered for the services witnessed the wedding, all who cared to stay.

"My wedding dress was a dark blue, trimmed in white lace about an inch wide. The material was heavy, sort of a weave. I wanted a light blue, but my mother went to town and bought the material. She never knew I was disappointed. The groom got a suit if he could afford it, if not he wore what he had. People did not go in debt for things they wanted. If there was no money, you didn't buy it."

Mrs. Pruitt explained that Henry's proposal was not the only part of their wedding that went a little shaky. "We were to be married on our front porch. What a beautiful night, something old, something new, friends and relations gathered all around. Now, the great moment! The porch fell down! There was bedlam for a while, but the vows were exchanged, and suspecting a shivaree, Henry and I spent the night in the Tunnel of Love."

Homes served as the site for most social activity, and parties alternated from one to another. Games were played and the proper spin of a bottle might secure a companion for a stroll around the house in the dark. There is, however, evidence that at least one high stepping game was improvised.

Some years ago at the Farmers Market Café in Greenville, I worked on bacon, eggs, and steaming coffee. Outside a chill wind whistled. A loose windowpane rattled. The small café was packed. A table of local old-timers blew on their coffee, slapped each other on the back, and enjoying tales of the old days.

I couldn't help but overhear, even if I'd wanted. I didn't. The times they glorified were those bygone days when light bulbs hung on a cord from high ceilings and it took two hands, one to steady it and the other to turn the switch, to operate them.

"Yeah," one said, "we walked everywhere in them days. Why, I wouldn't think nothing of walking six miles to get to a party."

"You remember old Racehorse Willis?" another asked.

All admitted knowing Racehorse. "Wasn't he something. Kick higher than anybody I ever knew." The speaker had a girth that suggested forty years of insurance sales and a squat stature that explained his long envy of high steppers.

A red-faced man in overalls put down his saucer. "He could kick high. Saw Charlie bet him four bits once he couldn't kick high enough to touch the light."

"I 'member that. That 'uz at Sally Mae Silvers party wasn't it."

The red-faced man nodded.

"Did Racehorse do it?" the salesman asked.

"Made Charlie double his bet then he collected the money by kicking the light out behind his back—backwards."

Murmurs of understanding mixed with chuckles circled the little table then silence. Each of the five men grew solemn and wagged their heads while examining the depths of their cups.

The first speaker took a deep breath. "Times were hard back then."

"Thing was, there wasn't no money," said the good hands man.

"We'ud starved one year if it hadn't been for sweet taters and hickory nuts," said the man in overalls.

A twinkle lit the eye of the insurance man. "Let me tell you. It was so poor around our house one Christmas the boys that hadn't reached puberty had nothing to play with."

I sensed the coffee come up past my throat and burn my sinuses. I groped for a napkin. The old-timer's table was in an uproar. The waitress ducked her head and did a U-turn back into the kitchen. After collecting myself I looked at the next table. Tears streamed down cheery faces and all eyes were on the insurance salesman.

A few minutes later, I drove out of town through drizzle and heavy clouds. I thought of the brightness those old-timers had added to that cramped little space. For me they'd been a treat.

Perhaps there was life after credit cards, traffic lights, office politics, and quarterly reviews. Maybe we, too, had a chance at grace.

I thought of one of my grandmothers, married at sixteen, widowed at forty-eight, and never remarrying. It seems a paradox that most young people grow larger today, yet move into the adult world at a later age. Certainly, the age of consent for marriage was lower in 1900 than today and most entered the work force earlier. Still, divorce was rare, almost unheard of.

Some say it was a simpler time. I find no evidence to support that assumption. There was less information, fewer things, and more physical activity. There was also more creativity. Almost all essentials, tools, toys, and homes required creation. Still, even with less time it seems they had more fun. Fortunately for all of us, with those good people, the two went together.

Signs, Hijinks, and Superstition

The sailors at Galveston weren't the only Texans to watch nature's book for signs. Mrs. Casey offered an example of the attention people of Brown County gave such events. "Back in the early 1930s Sam Parks, an old bachelor uncle, came to spend a week with mother and me in Brown County. A cattle buyer named Frank Lacy came by to look at some stock and, as was the custom, to spend the night. There had been a long dry spell, and the two men were on the porch discussing the weather.

"Lacy said, 'You know, we've got the best chance in the world for rain. It is the time of the equinox, the points of the moon are down to pour out water, and there is a cloud in the east.'

"Sam agreed and added that he had killed a snake that morning and hung it over the fence, which should help. The cloud came up with thunder and lightning then broke up and blew off.

"Frank said, 'When it's dry like this all good signs fail.'"

Bedi Taylor, of Colorado City, would tell you in a minute he got rid of the old ways just as fast as he could find a new one. He took to all things electrical like a pup to milk, especially radio. Before the ink was dry on the first repair manual, he'd mastered the course. He pioneered radio sales and installation west of Fort Worth and repaired them in the back of his hardware store in Colorado City for many years. Some of those old ways just would not scrub off, though.

Like most towns in West Texas's farm belt, the local merchants faced difficult years in the sixties and seventies as populations moved to the cities and farms became bigger. Discount stores popped up, highways improved, and about that time TV cut down on the Saturday night crowd. With the appearance of video, radio repair declined. All these things combined to hurt Bedi a little at the cash register, but he wasn't complaining—it wasn't his way.

One Friday evening in the 1960s as I leaned on one counter and Mr. Taylor another, and after two hours without a customer, a man from the Spade Ranch, south of town, came in and asked Bedi if he would look at his old radio.

"Just set her down on the counter and I'll have her for you next week," Mr. Taylor said.

L. J. "Bedi" Taylor (standing).

After a few minutes discussing the dry weather and the Wolves' last game, the rancher bid us "so-long" and departed. Bedi filled out a ticket and tied it around the cord to the radio, wrapped the cord around the whole thing, and sat it on his workbench.

Earlier, a car had parked two blocks away, but I didn't see any sign of a rush for the store's front door. We'd already killed most of the day, and I figured if Bedi knew he did not have to entertain his kid son-in-law, he'd be anxious get some work done.

"You probably want to get started on that radio so I'll just go on up to the house."

"I can't," he said.

I looked around. "Why?"

"It's Friday. We don't start new jobs on Friday, bad luck you know." Bedi used "we" when someone asked for credit or when explaining a backorder item's lateness in arriving from Amarillo Hardware. Otherwise, he ran pretty much a one-man show.

Mr. Taylor found it no more difficult to rid himself of his old-time superstitions than the people of Amarillo did their fear of Indians.

"News arrived in Amarillo in 1891 that Indians on the war-path had attacked and burned the town of Memphis, killing and scalping the men, women, and children.

"Judge Holland said that it was in the air; had he not seen Indian smoke sign for several days issuing from Palo Duro Can-yon, rising straight up, such as only Indians could produce?

"People all over the Panhandle were alarmed. They began pouring into town. Amarillo became full of excited people. Guns were ready for use. Canyon's citizens dug trenches, housed the children and womenfolk in the courthouse, and prepared for war. Claude and other surrounding towns organized for war-fare, and Clarendon, indeed the most courageous of all, prepared to send armed relief to the aid of Memphis. However, before this was done, to the relief of all, the truth was discovered. It was found that the smoke, which had produced the alarm, resulted from a prairie fire, and Memphis was unharmed."

Carrying the name of a great uncle who was father of humorist Will Rogers, Clem "Doc" Reynolds settled as a boy on a ranch near Canyon. The Indians were gone when he got there, but he did encounter his share of eagles. "The older boys made us afraid to be out on a horse alone, because they said an eagle would swoop down and catch us and carry us off.

"One time two of my brothers and I found an eagle's nest in a hole on the bank of the canyon. Cecil tied a rope around his foot and took a pitchfork. Stix and I were supposed to hold the rope and let him down to rake the little eagle out. Just about the time he raked at the eagle the rope slipped, and the eagle fell about a hundred feet, into a hackberry tree. We got him for a pet, and he could eat two jackrabbits a day. He didn't always get 'em, but he could eat that much."

Panhandle native G. L. Browning remembered. "Old Man Wallace, who settled at Washburn in '88, conceived the idea of building a sail wagon to travel over these plains. He came here from California with lots of experience with sailboats. He sent to St. Louis and had a light spring wagon made and shipped out to Washburn. Then he rigged a sail and steering gear.

"I knew he was building this thing, this sail wagon. One day on land I took up, I was plowing two little mustang ponies, trying to break some land. I looked up the road and saw a big white sail fluttering in the air, pulling the sail wagon on its maiden voyage.

"Well, I saw this thing coming, and the old man run down the side of the road and stopped. He got out and walked over to me and says, 'Browning, the wind's getting pretty high and I haven't got my sail so I can reef her, and I'm about to turn over. I need some weight on this wagon.'

"He says, 'You know there's no rocks I can get here to put in as ballast, and I don't have a sack to fill with dirt, so come and get in and go to Amarillo with me.'

"I says, 'Well, Mr. Wallace, I been plowing three days, and if you had a sack I haven't got enough dirt plowed to fill one, so I'll turn 'em loose here in the field and go with you.' And a wild ride we had to the old town of Amarillo. We passed telegraph poles so fast that they looked as close together as the teeth of a fine comb.

"A fellow from Louisiana, who was new, had just settled on the Kilgore land near the road. He saw us coming. He got his family together and said, 'Let's get inside; we don't know what these people got out here in this country.' He went in and closed all the doors, saying later, 'The damn thing sounded like the clatter wheels of hell.'

"Well, we run on down into the old town and turned into the main business block there. Fifteen or twenty cowponies was hitched to the rack in front of the business houses. Not being used to such machinery they all broke loose, except one who looked like he was going to die in the rack.

"The businesses all suspended. Everybody come out and surrounded the new mode of travel. They passed judgement on it. Some said it would never do. We faced about and went back home."

Between Indian scares, eagles, and sail wagons, you might think that the inhabitants of the Panhandle region had little time to build, but the fact is some of the greatest ranches in Texas heated their irons there. Over in Randall County the T Anchor ($\underline{\text{T}}$) Ranch is known for many records and firsts in Western lore. It claims to be the home of the first hand-hewn log building in the Panhandle, the first crop of oats, and the first irrigation.

Log buildings, oats, and irrigation are okay for men with their feet on the ground, but the old boys wearing spurs like to strut their stuff and tell that the T Anchor also holds the record for the largest number of cattle ever driven in one herd, 10,650 head. Certainly, that gets everyone's attention, but in the eyes of many, a letter written to one of the outfit's cowboys, back in the early days, set a mark for caring that will never be broken.

"A drive to Ft. Reno, Oklahoma, contributed one of the most widely known tales of the T Anchor drive. Some of the boys wrote home that they were going into Indian Territory. One boy received the following letter, which the other hands got and read in his absence."

> Dear Bub,
>
> I don't want you to go where those old Indians are. They might scalp you, and if they did, I would surely die. Be careful Bub, and don't let them hurt you, because you are the roasting-ears of my heart and the cornbread of my existence.

In early Texas, the word rabies matched Indian, superstition, or eagle, as a frightful word. Mothers sometimes used its image as a questionable method of discipline for unruly children. "You behave or we'll put you out with that old mad dog (bull or whatever the latest rumor supported)." This threat alone was enough to curdle the demons from the most rambunctious child and send chills up the backs of adults.

South Texas, in particular, seemed to provide favorable conditions for hydrophobia. An oil discovery in Harris County at a place called Moonshine Hill created an early boomtown. A local barber practiced medicine on the side. One day while the doctor was in back with a patient, two men waited. One was ill the other needed a shave.

A rabies epidemic dominated the conversation around the rigs at that time. The man waiting for the barber work asked the other, an acquaintance, what his ailment was since it was obvious the man hurt. The ill roughneck seized the opportunity, drooled slightly out the mouth, and when the doctor appeared he found one customer "treed" on a barber's chair and the other down on the floor on his all fours. Roughnecks like lumberjacks, cowboys, and farmers had need of an occasional good laugh.

Booming Towns and Gushing Oil

Gold took the Forty-niners to California, spawned roaring boomtowns, then beckoned from the cold north. Cattle markets gave birth to wild end-of-trail towns at Abilene, Dodge, and other sites in the Midwest. Legends of wealth and rowdiness fought for center stage. Then came oil.

At one time the mention of powerful moguls brought to mind visions of oil framed in an outline of Texas. In the old days and with oil a new industry, as soon as the state developed one area of production another discovery would occur. Men with courage and luck and a nature inclined toward risk-taking often became overnight millionaires. For a few, this new stature lasted, for more it was a fleeting experience.

Most found wealth harder to maintain than to achieve. Texas had almost as bottomless a source of these kinds of men as she did for the oil they hunted. Even more important she had strong men willing to fill the needs of the many hard and dangerous occupations required by the new fields of toil. Often more courageous, stronger, and more loyal than the men who paid them, they risked their lives while the owner risked his wealth. Motivated by near poverty and the needs of loved ones, they gave no quarter and asked none. Hard, tough, coarse, chasing a good wage and a better tomorrow, they lived in a time

119

when opportunity existed. Some rose from the black mud to the heady heights of oilman then moved on, gathering support to push their own wildcat into the depths.

During the first half of the twentieth century, in war and peace, Texas provided the raw material for a good portion of our nation's energy needs. Good schools, state facilities, and a healthy tax base repaid her. None of it—not one trickle of oil—would have been made available without the vital accomplishments of the last of the old-time Texans and others like them.

Hayne Sheffield wrote, "The earliest account of the use of oil in America is found in the recording of the De Soto expedition of 1543. Four of his ships sought shelter from a storm by sailing into Sabine Pass on the Texas coast. They found, floating on the water's surface, a thick scum of oil, similar to pitch, which was used to caulk ships in Spain. To their amazement, this oil, which they called 'cope,' proved effective in stopping leaks when applied to the bottom of their ships.

"C. E. Barrett discovered the first oil at Humble, Texas, in 1904." The site of the discovery was Moonshine Hill.

"Excitement in Humble reached a feverish peak on the morning of January 8, 1905. D. R. Beatty completed the first gusher at Humble. His number 2 well on block 28 of the Long subdivision was producing at a rate of 13,000 barrels of oil per day. The long-sought-after caprock had finally been tapped at 1,012 feet.

"In an interview with a reporter, he remarked that he had shown a net profit of $50,000 the first thirty days, even though he was receiving only eighteen cents per barrel for the sale of the oil."

Mrs. Poly Archer's family moved to Humble a decade later, during the second boom. She said, "The four of us lived, slept, cooked, and ate in the one room. We came to Humble from Normangee, Texas. Being the first ones of either of my parents' families to leave the farming country, others thought we were going to starve. I remember hearing that Alma and Edgar were, 'way down there with those children, living out of a paper sack.'"

Mary and Henry Pruitt never resided in a paper sack at Humble, but Mary said, "My sister, Lil, and her husband, Will Owens, lived in a tent that had board sides that could be raised at night to take advantage of any breeze that might be blowing. One night Lil was lying in bed with her arm thrown over her head when someone took the rings off her fingers. Fearing for her life, she pretended to sleep and never attempted to prevent the rings from being stolen."

Oil was not the only cause of boomtowns in the early twenties. Good farm land and the extension of rail spurs often made for rapid growth. Bomarton in Baylor County expanded rapidly about that time. A new generation was preparing to come of age, but the frontier and individualism had deep roots.

Sid Murdock had made another move west and this time settled in Bomarton. Dad, now about fourteen, had discovered ice cream.

"Doc Gaines was a local doctor there in Bomarton," Dad said. "He and his brother owned a drugstore. A friend, I think his name was Thurmon or Furman Akridge and I were in there at the counter one day eating a cone.

"Well, this man comes up the sidewalk weaving a little and mumbling something. Doc Gaines sort of waved us toward the rear of the store with his arm. 'You boys move back over here,' he said. We did, and by this time the man, his name was a Mr. Hartsell, stood outside, even with the drugstore screen door. He peeked in and mumbled some more, I think he was sort of singing a little song, or a saying, or something.

"Anyway, by this time Doc Gaines stood inside the screen and he had a shotgun in his hand. He raised that gun and pointed it right at that man's chest. Bam! Right through that screen door, he shot him."

"His brother put his hand on Doc's shoulder and said, 'That's enough, Doc, come on back.'

"Mr. Hartsell had turned and ran. His pickup was middle ways of the street. We later learned he fell dead right at his truck."

"What did you do?" I asked.

"We were out that back door and didn't stop till we got home."

"What was it about?" I asked.

"I never knew. I guess the grownups had some idea, but I never knew. They held a trial I think. I was back in Wood County at that time, but I think they called the other boy to testify. If Doc Gaines served any time, though, it wasn't much."

Nova Bair's family lived on a farm near Amarillo. Her family loaded a covered wagon and moved to Burkburnett, another oil boom in 1917. "I was just past six years old. My brother and I rode horses and drove Daddy's loose teams that he planned to

Burkburnett as an oil boomtown.
Photo courtesy Texas State Library and Archives Commission

put to work in the oil fields. We lived in tents for some time after we arrived in Burkburnett."

Staunch people, those who survived were tempered by the conditions of the time. Dorthy Smith McLin wrote, "I was born March 4, 1919, on Jordon Gulley. Dr. Dameron came from Humble to deliver me. He told my sister, Louise, he brought me from Belgium in his little black bag. She had a lot of fun at school the next day telling of the little Belgian baby."

Oil patch greenhorns from the ranches, farms, and sawmills of Texas following the lure of steady pay into the oil fields found openings numerous. All the jobs were dangerous. Whether a man ended up on a drilling crew, mule skinning, working as a rigger, or as a pipe liner, his primary safety aid was an ability to sense danger and move quickly when disaster struck. Lives and limbs were the victims of fires, explosions, ruptured lines, broken chains and cables as well as falling derricks and objects. Wheels, sprockets, and flywheels were mostly unguarded.

Life was as precious then as today, but it was certainly much cheaper. Workman's compensation laws, hard hats, Ralph Nader, and civil recourse were generations away. Each worker accepted the dangers knowing a day's pay for a day of work was the best he could hope for. He took the job with pride, giving the boss man both his loyalty and his energy.

Personal traits and characteristics quickly stuck as nicknames, and some were not complimentary. Snuffy, Nubby, Shorty, Flap, and Lefty might appear on either a paycheck or a bar bill. Flap might limp, Nubby would likely only have one hand, and Snuffy might have a dirty chin. Still, a thick skin served a man well, and the one assigning the less-than-complimentary title might end up a most loyal friend.

As often as not "a cussing" took precedence over employee training and no one held immunity. Nevertheless, personal boundaries were respected. A hungry man might take being likened to a mule with a few colorful and profane adjectives sprinkled in, but questioning one's personal courage or parentage was going a step too far. Demeaning the character of a sister or lady friend's virtue invited a fight, and even the toughest bully was vulnerable on the narrow unlit boardwalks at night.

Often a new well site resulted as much from luck or accident as from planning. I drank coffee recently with a shallow well stripper who worked his way through many an early Texas boomtown. We were in Olney at the time. Fred is the only name I caught. "I've seen oilmen take the last drink then throw an empty whiskey bottle backward over their shoulder and spend the next several weeks drilling where she fell. Other times I've seen 'em get stuck in mud trying to get to a particular spot and just start drilling. Sometimes they were dry, others they brought 'em in."

When a new field opened or a site for an exploratory well, a wildcat, was selected, the first on the scene was the muleskinner. Exhibiting both the art of a conductor and the profanity of a sailor, he and his animals worked in harmony and precision. Loads of timber for the derrick, its floor, and outbuildings were brought in. Instances are recorded where muddy fields required teams of as many as forty-eight mules to deliver heavy boilers to the site. The crack of the teamster's whip and the shouted names of his animals could be heard above the busiest field.

Rig builders assembled the bracing lumber to the sturdy timber used for derrick legs, built the outbuildings, and set heavy machinery onto semipermanent bases. Using hatchets for both nail driving and timber forming, they were specialists, and a good team could erect an 86-foot derrick in a day.

The "day tower" and the "graveyard tower" each lasted twelve hours and with the two drilling crews that worked them kept the rigs running constantly. A crew consisted of five men, the driller and his four roughnecks.

Haynes Sheffield wrote, "The pot fireman never had enough steam; the derrick man ran the pump and performed all work above the derrick floor. The pipe racker worked the educated side of the rotary and the 'bo-weevil' on the other side."

After production was obtained, the pipe-liners made their appearance. They claimed to be able to "cuss louder, lie better, fight longer, drink more liquor, and work harder than any other group of men in the field. Made up mostly of young unmarried men, they considered it their duty to support the local saloon. Having established credit for their bar bill and the other niceties provided on the premises, their conversation ranged from the new girl at the saloon to snuff-dipping Anne, who lived near the mule barn. They worked during the day and prowled all night. Good at their jobs, they only asked for enough pipe and a direction to plant it."

As the new shift's work began and stiff muscles loosened, the tempo quickened and sounds rose to a crescendo. Men with more strength than patience yelled commands, nearby freight trains shrieked, and every piece of equipment on dozens of nearby rigs banged, creaked, hissed, or rattled. Fires roared in boiler fireboxes. Mules brayed and their masters cracked whips into rifle-like explosions.

Mr. Sheffield continued, "Texas's oil industry began near the famous oil springs of Angelina County in 1859. Later, the discovery of the Corsicana oilfield was accidental. In 1894 the city of Corsicana was drilling a water well, when, at a depth of 1,020 feet, oil was discovered. Two years later three hundred wells were in production, pipeline and tank storage had been installed, a modern refinery was in operation, and the local market for the refined products was expanding.

"The discovery of oil at Spindletop, near Beaumont, produced madness in man never exhibited before in our nation. On January 10, 1901, the Lucas gusher roared in at 75,000 barrels per day. Acre tracts near the well were sold at $900,000." The market was glutted. Soon oil was being stored in open pits. The price fell to three cents a barrel."

Mr. Sheffield added, "Historians should be charged with neglect for their failure to record the first sale of oil, because it was this sale that produced two 'firsts' to an industry yet unborn: 'profit' and 'rip-off.' Oil in its unrefined state has no intrinsic value, hence the 'rip-off,' however the very fact it could be sold introduced the first profit motive."

Noise and excitement accentuated opportunity. Knee-deep mud and the odor of oil, sweat, and sulfur, plus the smell of 2,000 mules brought home reality. The boomtown had it all. Men's suits at $9.95, lady's dresses at $2, and 10 yards of piece goods at $.49 were examples of the exorbitant inflation that followed the good times. Yet, here was a way of life that lured many for year after year, a special music for special people.

Snakes, Pests, and Bandits

Mother squeezed off another shot. Bang! She held the six-shooter in both hands—hands that shook. Bang! Her shots punctuated the loud whirring, rattling sound—the sound of death, coming from near the edge of the house's foundation. She stood on the concrete sidewalk six feet from the front door and a similar distance from the writhing diamondback. With the impact of each of the .38 slugs entering its coiled body, the snake lashed out, striking at air. Bang! Splinters flew from the siding covering the foundation of the house ten inches from the snake. Mom lowered the pistol and turned and placed it on the porch. She sat beside it, shaking, watching the snake's death struggle.

She had lived up to the unwritten creed that all in our immediate neighborhood shared. "If you see a rattler, kill it!" She showed me the bullet hole in the house when I visited home from college. We teased her some, gave her our manly advice about more effective weapons for snake killing, like hoes, shotguns, .22 rifles, but it was half-hearted. We were all in awe of her spunk and proud of her.

Snakes and thorns have been responsible for two pieces of apparel for which Texas is famous, chaps and boots. Few areas offer both pests more plentifully than the bordering brake areas of the rivers of West Texas. Living among them develops, in most of us, a little paranoia. You tend to jump when waiters rustle change by your shoulder. A fine trigger remains cocked inside your reaction system, ready to go off at any sudden movement or sound. You never outgrow this.

Jack Spann had a touch of snake country upbringing before going to the South Pacific during the last world war. Like snakes from parts of East Texas, those over there gave no warning before striking. Jack had a shelter hole that the insects, vermin, and snakes liked better than he did.

Another acquaintance that routinely dropped by Jack's hole was a Japanese Zero his outfit had tagged "Washing Machine Charlie." When the Zero or any of its buddies came over, Spann did battle for possession of his bomb shelter.

Jack said, "We had an air raid alert and they were overhead pretty quickly. It was night, dark as pitch and lights-out were standing orders when under attack. I'd not had time to check that hole before I jumped in, and no sooner had things got quiet than I knew I had company. When there was no noise and things were still, I could sense more than hear the movement in there—man! Soon as they removed the alert, I turned on my flashlight. It was just a sand crab."

Paul Carter, an aircraft mechanic in the Army Air Corps, also experienced unwelcome guests in his foxhole. Both he and Jack served on the island of New Guinea. Paul remembered, "Leaves would fall down in those holes and it was cooler down there than on higher ground. They had, I believe we called it, a black adder snake that was supposed to be the most poisonous snake in the world. Well, those things liked to crawl down in those holes and cool off under the leaves. You had to watch out for them."

Snakes in South and West Texas at least announce their presence. The coral, the copperhead, and the moccasin of the eastern part of the state are less considerate. The area of Galveston and its surrounding marshlands is notorious for its snake population. Dr. David McComb wrote that early maps

Sgt. Paul L. Carter on right at Everett, Washington
in December 1941. His companion on the left is
Lt. Albert W. Schinz of Korean War fame.

designate the eastern tip of Galveston Island as the "point of the
Snakes."

He adds, "In the mid-1900s as many as twenty to thirty people are still treated at the University of Texas Medical Branch
each year for snakebite.

"In 1964 Willie Burns, chief of the Galveston Police at the
time, was at home while his wife worked in the garden. She
screamed, 'Willie, it's a rattlesnake! Don't move! Call the police!'

"'Why should I call the police? I am the chief of police.' With
that pronouncement and a rake he killed the snake."

An unwritten law along the Salt Fork of the Brazos is that a
man worth his salt kills his own snakes. For some that is more

difficult than for others. A middle-aged neighbor just could not handle that part of manhood. He sought help each time he found a rattler. Frequently this meant the snake disappeared with his venom intact while this farmer drove the couple of miles after reinforcements.

A serious case of insecurity must result upon realizing that a healthy rattler, seen a few minutes earlier on the top step of the storm cellar, has escaped, particularly if clouds are forming.

At some point, I learned the snake-fearing man's brother had agitated this fright since childhood. He delighted in telling of his younger brother's panic upon looking to his rear and spotting the chain he pulled with his own shoulder through tall grass. Another of his favorite stories concerned earlier days and his covering a small rope with dirt in the milk shed and slipping up and pulling it beneath the little brother's milk stool. It would be nice if the younger man was able to even-up the score, but life and snakes don't always play by the rules.

Almost as bad as snakes but less deadly were the ticks and chiggers of East Texas. They don't kill, but they make death less frightful.

A few years ago, my wife and I rode with my Uncle Wyman in his pickup. He crossed his beautiful hay fields, pointed out good fat cattle, and offered to show us how he fed his pond-raised catfish. Wyman retired to Canton and was back among the piney woods of his youth. In any crowd, this uncle was one of Joanne's favorites and she wanted very much to keep the conversation going. She also had fresh memories of some of our own farm-raised pets from a few miles up the road.

"Do you have ticks or chiggers?" Joanne asked.

"Got both," Wyman replied laughingly. "Which do you want?" He continued on and showed us how his pond-raised fish boiled the water, impatient for food when he rattled a bucket. Watching them brought visions of hushpuppies and fried catfish.

While ticks and chiggers in large doses can be dangerous, normally they aren't. Combined with other insects, they do cause considerable expense to the livestock industry. However, the real economic damage from insects in Texas comes from those enemies of cotton, primarily the boll weevil. By the mid-twentieth century this pest had accounted for chasing the cotton belt west from the southern states and East Texas and into arid regions of the west. Today millions, perhaps billions, of dollars are being spent by federal and local agriculture organizations to combat this menace.

Uncle George Harvey of Dickens County talked of insects. "The year 1893 started as a good year," he said. "There was enough moisture in the ground to bring up the grain crops, cane, maize, and corn. When these crops got about waist high the drought struck. The cane began to twist, and the people looked skyward. Then one morning to their dismay they looked out on their crops and discovered an army of grasshoppers had literally covered the fields. They were destroying everything in their path. They marched, flew, devoured, and climbed the stalks of grain, one behind the other until their weight bent the stalk to the ground; then the head-hoppers would move to another stalk and in the same manner destroy it. They set a straight course from east to west, not varying their direction. It was a year never to be forgotten."

One success story of man's war against harmful insects is the recent control, almost total eradication, of the screw worm fly. The larva of this fly at one time menaced Texas ranchers as well as the big game industry in the state. This larva formed from an egg deposited by the fly in open wounds on livestock, deer, and other animals. Today a fly sterilization program has freed Texas of this pest. Large wild animal populations, such as hogs and deer, have benefited from this program, as well as ranchers' herds. Though it contributes infrequently to the food source today, revenue from hunting is big business.

In the earliest decades of the century, game provided a portion of the menu. Dependent upon the locale and the situation with each family, this practice slowed to a stop at varying times across the state. Prior to this, however, many of the larger animals had been wiped out in Texas. First of the wild animals to go, and before the period of the last of our old-time Texans, were the buffalo. Next were the elk. Shortly behind them, and about the time of the beginning of our current period, the herds of antelope disappeared and the bear and the panther weren't far behind.

Grandmother Jackson spent her early years near Weatherford. However, Granddad arrived in Knox County in 1889, when he was about seven. Granny once told me, "I never saw many antelope, but Jim could remember herds of them crossing near the home place."

Not only did those earlier old-timers gather much of their food from the wild, but parents taught them how to use game and domestic animals for a variety of utensils about the home. For many years Granny's house sported cowhide covered straight-back chairs. Colorful, with the hair intact, they were comfortable. A hunting horn given as a Christmas present prompted Granny to a story of her youth.

"Let me see that." She reached for the horn's leather thong.

Taking the horn she examined it closely. "I used to help Poppa make these. You see, you take a piece of glass then find a cow's horn. After a period of time that inner part of the horn can be reamed out, and you take the outer part and scrape it with the edge of the glass until it shines just like this one."

I stepped through Christmas wrappings to her side and took the horn and tried to make a sound with it. She laughed. "Poppa had a hunting horn he took when he and the dogs went hunting. He'd blow it to call the dogs in after the hunt."

"You all lived near Parker County then, didn't you?" My second effort with the horn increased my embarrassment.

Granny retrieved the horn and laughed. She fondled it. She stroked it, checking its smoothness. "When he wasn't hunting he kept his horn by the door to be used as an alarm signal while the men were away in the fields. Momma or one of the older children could blow it and alert the menfolks. It was not to be played with."

"I wanted to blow that thing so bad. I would slip it down when they were away and try and try. Well one day I made a beautiful full-blown call. The men were away across the field and I looked out and they were all coming on a dead run. I knew I was in trouble."

"Did you get a spanking?"

"I think he just raised the peg and put the horn higher on the door."

Later, thinking of this use of a cow's horn, I recalled the old expression describing active or mischievous people. "They'll build a spoon or spoil a horn." For the first time, I realized the saying was literal and horns, no doubt, served as the raw material for spoons as well as alarms in earlier days.

Carl Nicholson started hunting during the second decade of this century. He said, "What I shot generally ended up on the table. Rabbits, squirrel, and all kinds of edible fowl made up a good part of our menu. We weren't that different than the pioneers before us."

Vivian Hess grew up near Josephine in Hunt County and remembers World War II hero Audie Murphy. She said, "Much of his family's meals before he went into the army came from what he shot. I'm sure that helped make him a good marksman and become our most decorated hero."

Velma Nichols Short's family lived in Rains County. She wrote, "I can remember a story my father, Clark Nichols, told many times about when he and his cousin were twelve years old and squirrel hunting on the Sabine River bottom. They heard a panther scream and started running. When it screamed again, they dropped their guns and squirrels so they could run faster.

"When they arrived at his uncle's house, Uncle Griff said they had not heard a panther because there wasn't any in Rains County. Just before Uncle died, after my father was a grown man, he told him it was a panther they heard. He didn't want the boys to be afraid to go hunting and knew they would be if they had known it really was a panther."

At the end of the century these panthers, pumas, or mountain lions are making a comeback in the state. At one time pushed to the far reaches of the southwest mountainous region of Texas, the big cats were almost totally absent for over half a century. Now, thanks to that improving deer and wild hog population, sightings are occurring in even populated regions. Perhaps ticks are not so bad, after all.

Lobo wolves ravaged through the last decades of their destruction during the early 1900s in Dickens County. "Cattlemen in that area claimed a full-grown lobo, in cattle country, would likely kill fifteen or twenty head of cattle a year. The yearbook of the U.S. Department of Agriculture gave an account where an unusually wily lobo averaged killing fifty head a year for over five years, often killing cows for the sake of eating their unborn calves."

Jack Propps chased a few wolves two counties east of Dickens County, in Knox County. He remembered "taking a hard fall" chasing the last lobo wolves he saw in that area sometime after 1906. "The wolves crossed prairie dog town, later the A. L. Kinnibrough farm. We dug five pups from a den that day on the McCoo branch." According to Jack his effort netted him $50 a scalp bounty, paid by the county. Two hundred and fifty dollars for a day's work during a dollar-a-day economy would seem likely to draw a large following.

The Big Bend area may or may not have provided the incubator for the return of the pumas, but it certainly became the site of one of the stranger incidents in American history. This event dealt with bandits not panthers. In early January 1914, without ever having entered a war, U.S. Cavalrymen found themselves captors of an entire foreign army. The Mexican rebel leader Francisco (Pancho) Villa had the Mexican army whipped and ready for annihilation at Ojinaga, Mexico. It is the only time in the history of the United States that a nation's army sought safety by surrendering to neutral U.S. forces.

Described as "a scene of wild disorder," 2,175 Federal Mexican soldiers, 129 officers, and an estimated 1,500 civilian refugees and camp followers crossed the Rio Grande to Puerto Rico near the old customshouse in Presidio. Sick, hungry, cold, and panic-stricken, the group converged on 500 U.S. Cavalrymen. Bent on giving up their weapons, they begged for protection. They left behind scattered bodies and bitter defeat.

Forming a column twelve miles long and outnumbering their escort of soldiers by ten to one, the group later staggered to Marfa. One resident along the route recalled seeing the long straggling line of refugees as "...a pitiful sight, like cattle being herded up the road."

The refugees were ultimately shipped to El Paso by train; our neighbor to the south had once again found a way to test the social conscience of the time. Ladies of the Home Missionary Society, assisted by the Marfa Chamber of Commerce, campaigned for relief for this human suffering while others cautioned against aid, too liberal, that would induce an influx of "this class."

Far to the east our European neighbors prepared for war with Germany. Many in Texas also recognized the threat in that direction. For those few Texans scattered along our southwestern border, a more immediate danger lurked and demanded a wary eye be directed to the south. Bandit raids were not uncommon, and losses by Texas citizens occurred frequently; however, most Texans favored the cause of the insurgents as opposed to the dictatorial Federals.

Mr. H. D. Arnold taught and became school superintendent at Goree, in Knox County. In the forties he entertained a number of us with childhood memories. "We stood on railroad cars at the edge of El Paso and watched a battle rage between Pancho Villa and the Federal troops. The gunfire excited us and for the kids on our side of the river it was a great show, but we knew little of what it was about."

Tom Landry would have liked Mr. Arnold. He was the epitome of what an educator was expected to be during his era. Articulate, immaculate, and intelligent, he tolerated no nonsense. Still, no matter how rough your own edges, if you were his student, you knew he was on your side. And he was a teller of good stories, though he dispensed them judiciously.

At the time Mr. Arnold, as a boy, watched the activity south of the Rio Grande, only seventy-five years had passed since Texas had won its independence from Mexico. It was an independence fought for landholding residents and by immigrants from Tennessee, Louisiana, and other states, who were little interested in social class or government aid.

The writers of Marfa and Presidio County's history state, "An undocumented number of good citizens migrated to Presidio County from Mexico throughout the Revolution. Those whose names are listed represent but a small percentage of the total number who transferred their allegiance from Mexico to the United States in the period 1911-1920.

"Known as a 'maestro blacksmith,' Serapio U. Santos came to Shafter from Mexico in January 1911. He helped to design and construct the little train used to pull cars of ore from the mine to the mill in 1914.

"Jesus B. Ramos brought his family to Presidio in 1911. His daughter, Nina Ramos, was married to T. O. Jacques. She worked in the Presidio pharmacy and post office for many years.

"Anres Magallanes married Lucia Carrasco in Mulata, Chihuahua, then brought her to Redford during the revolution in 1911. Andres ranched between Redford and Lajitas and drove the mail from Lajitas to the Chisos mines. Later, in 1934, he moved to Shafter and purchased a moving picture theatre which his son operated."

Will Rogers tossed his rope along with his humor around the New York stages in those days. The great American humorist summed up the feelings of the times. He said, "I see by the headlines that Villa escapes net and flees. It seems the rebel is destined to remain free, for an army that can't catch fleas has no chance against such a man."

Many Texans of this day had little time to ponder the affairs of Mexico or Europe. The ways of bandits, fleas, and warlords were of little consequence when measured beside important issues like the right to drink, and keeping the little woman at home and out of the polls.

Prohibition and Bootlegger's Badges

T he humorist Will Rogers said, "I never met a man I didn't like."

His friend Charles Russell mentioned, "If I like a man when I'm sober, I kin hardly keep from kissing him when I'm drunk. This goes both ways. If I don't like a man when I'm sober, I don't want him in the same town when I'm drunk."

Many old-time Texans were like Russell, switch hitters on this subject of drink. Having batted from both sides of the plate by the time they reached voting age, most tended to business and avoided the bottle. However they continued to maintain a liberal view of the subject, and consensus seemed to favor maintaining the right to wet their whistle on occasion. One never knew when they might need to replace the bottle kept for medicinal purposes. With their natural distrust of lawyers and politicians, they were strongly opposed to Austin or Washington acting as umpire over their thirst.

One early Texas trail driver declared his ultimate accomplishment in his memoirs and put this feeling of independence and disdain for officialdom into focus. "After my days on the trail I settled down, and my wife and I raised five children that lived. One girl died as an infant. Of the five boys that lived, I'm happy to say not one ever served a day in the pen or the legislature."

A Collin County writer stated in their history that. "One of the earliest and most prevalent and disturbing factors concerning conduct among the pioneers of this county was excessive drinking; for it appears that the use of liquor was more generally tolerated in those days. On his way to Texas in 1854, a highly respected and wealthy farmer, preacher, and county official, who later organized a number of churches in Collin County, purchased a large quantity of supplies, including a barrel of whiskey, at Little Rock, Arkansas. It must be remembered, however, that it was thought to be an antidote for all the evils one might encounter on such a journey 'except Indians and high water.'"

McKinney's elder R. C. Horn added, "Whiskey was passed around at hog-killings, corn-huskings, log-rollings, harvesting, and other gatherings. At first there were no saloons in McKinney, but whiskey was sold by the gallon in grocery stores. Later, half the business houses on the east side of the square were saloons. On March 8, 1902, voters voted in prohibition, and thereafter the city remained dry."

Seventeen years later in DeWitt County, "Though 1,437 men to 788 men voted their opposition to prohibition and 1,706 to 689 opposed allowing women to vote in a county-wide election held May 24, 1919, the eighteenth and nineteenth United States Constitutional Amendments did not agree."

Most respectable family men would deny drinking at the beginning of the century but would hasten to add, "except for a toddy now and then." After prohibition, drinking became as clandestine a function as Protestant worship had been eighty-five years earlier. The whiskey bottle or jug left its throne in the kitchen or on the mantel and gained acquaintance with cottonseed and hay in the barn.

As a young lady growing up in Haskell, LaVern Cummins Regen witnessed these events. "A rather near neighbor, though not in our block, boasted of her cleverness in hiding whiskey in pepper sauce bottles and other such receptacles to keep her husband from drinking what she had on hand for medical emergencies. She needn't have been so concerned about her little supply. He kept a quart in our hay and came over each evening to check on our cow."

For many years Haskell was home to one of Texas's more famous saloons. It sported a swinging sign out front proclaiming its function. "Whiskey, the Road to Ruin." Modern Texans often justify their silliness and heavy expenses or high tax burden by arguing that the jobs created and the stimulus to business justifies the burden. After studying the Road to Ruin's history I found it passed on this basis. The saloon met the increased job requirement by employing a one-armed man to paint the original sign, and business is said to have prospered.

We can't say if poetic inspiration or a strong whiff of spirits stirred the poet who first penned the following descriptive verses about Haskell's saloon.

A bar to joy which home imparts.
A door to tears and aching hearts;
A door to Heaven, a door to hell,
Who'ever named 'er, named 'er well.

Hollywood must have shot the scene a million times. Mrs. Beach, her husband, and a man named Will lived it. Thanks to Rosa Lee Wylie and friends of Van Horn, I now know it's true. The scene I speak of is when the bad guy gets "high in his cups" draws his gun, and after riding his horse into the store, fires at a hapless bystander's feet while demanding the innocent dance.

Ms. Wylie wrote, "The evil of the drink habit had its effect. Will Formwalt got drunk and rode his horse into the Beach Mercantile Company Store; no one could get him out. Mrs. Beach said she could, so she went in and ordered him out."

"He asked. 'Can you dance?'

"She said. 'No!'

"He said, 'Well, this is one time you will.' So he began to shoot at her feet. She ran across the street and he was right after her.

"Poor Mr. Beach was very scared, and all that he could do was yell. 'Run, Rose, run!' Fortunately, she was not hit."

Getting the first of the scene as accurate as they do, I suppose Hollywood is justified in taking some liberty with the hero's part, but prohibition just didn't work. Crime flourished and the consumption of alcohol increased. Bootlegging became big business and even after repeal of prohibition did well in dry counties. The roaring twenties tore at the fabric of a puritan America and put a romantic aura around deception and crime. Cheating became acceptable and, who knows, perhaps this was the era of conception that reincarnated itself in the me-first attitude so marked in the 1960s and '70s.

Whiskey and corn are only a few processes apart, so it may have been talk of whiskey that reminded Doyle Conine of corn, anyway, he chuckled to himself. "I hired a man down in central Texas near the little town of West once. It was a road construction job and I put him to work on putting out the flares around the construction site and filling the pots with kerosene and taking care of them. It was a good job and he had it because his house and field adjoined the highway. He only worked a few hours in the morning and a few hours in the evening.

"I noticed pretty soon he wasn't too fond of work, but he was close. Wal, this one day I noticed someone out in his field gathering corn. Just the team and this one person were working. I hadn't seen my man this day. The field worker came close enough, and I noticed it was a woman. She moved on finally to the backside of the field and I heard something and looked up and here came my man on a motorcycle. He went on past and down the road a little ways to a beer joint and in a little while came back by and stopped. We talked about this and that, and I noticed he kept sneaking glances at his wife way off out there almost out of sight. Directly he jumped on his bike and said, 'I better go, she's getting pretty close to the house.'"

An aversion to work and an affinity for strong drink, when combined, create a heavy drain on an industrious generation toiling in even a state rich in resources. After a few drinks at least one Texan was known to subscribe to the philosophy of, "No Siree, I ain't afraid of work—why I can lay down and sleep right beside it."

An old-timer who spent time cowboying in Randall County learned to regret his adoption of that code. An acquaintance told how it happened. "We had these steers in a round pen and one of the Block cowboys was lying on the ground drunk. We had worked these cattle all evening and none of them had stepped on him. Finally, we had one steer we could not get down. The ol' drunk roused and said, 'I'll get him, boys.'

"As he staggered over, the steer hooked him. The horn hit him at the bottom of the ribs and went up. I might have imagined it, but I swear it sounded like somebody rubbing a thumbnail up a washboard. It didn't hurt him, but we got him out of the pen."

After the repeal of prohibition a good part of Texas remained dry under local option laws for many years. Carl Nicholson was a printer throughout a good portion of the first half of this century and remembered an item printed while he worked on the staff of the Quitman paper in 1945. The item concerned a recent visit of the Liquor Control Board officers to that town. It stated. "Five moonshine stills were seized and destroyed and thirty-one bootleggers were arrested." Nicholson added, "But it only took a few weeks for the supply of liquor to return to normal."

I have some great-uncles that are near Dad's age. They were raised near Quitman. One came and lived with Dad's family a few weeks in West Texas. It would have been near 1927. "Yeah, Garver came out to pull bolls one year and lived with us in Knox County," Dad said.

"Cecil [Dad's older brother] got into a fight with an older man that was living in Poppa's shack. This man and his about-grown son were pulling bolls for us. They left some cotton on short rows, and Cecil told them to finish them out before the trailer was moved. Well, the old man called 'Cec' a liar and said those rows weren't theirs.

"The two of them went together, but Cecil could hold his own with most men, even then. This old man's big son stood maybe an inch taller than Garver and started to mix in it. Garver reached over and stopped him and said, 'Boy, you better not get in that, you might get hurt.'" Dad was eighty-nine when he told this story, but it had lost none of its luster.

"Where were you?" I asked.

"I don't know, over in the field somewhere. Anyway I thought Poppa was gonna blow up when he heard about it. He went down to that shack and told that man not to let daylight catch him on his place."

"So, how long did Garver stay out here?" I asked.

"Aw, soon as the crop was gathered, he had a pocket full of money and was ready to go back to Wood County. He did stop in Goree that night though to say so-long to some of those boys over there.

"I heard about it later. They had a little beer and along about midnight the constable took old Garver out to that little one-room jail sitting in the middle of the park over there and put him in it." Dad grinned.

"Garver said he woke up the next morning and that place didn't smell very good and he felt worse. Said he laid there on that little old cot and directly the constable cracked the door and peeked in.

"'You still here?' he asked.

"'Shore as hell am! You put me here, you know.'

"'Yeah, but I didn't lock the door.'" Dad chuckled as he finished.

During prohibition, Sheriff Schuyler Marshall Jr. tried hard to keep his territory in Dallas County law abiding. He said. "In my first two-year term, my office seized 309 stills, thousands of gallons of illicit liquor and mash, and arrested more than a thousand violators of the prohibition law."

A nearby Mesquite, Texas observer reported that, "Bootleggers were so thick at the Mesquite Fair they wore badges to keep from trying to sell to each other."

The Texas *Mesquiter* reported, "A man accused of bootlegging retorted defensively, 'Aint no way I can get enough ahead to sell. Hic!'"

At the nation's markets the high rollers copied each others' purchases and slapped each other on the back while shoeshine boys learned to read ticker tapes. Social excesses spilled into business judgements, and Texans began to feel their mother nation shake with economic jitters.

Selling was the vocation of the decade. Insurance companies sent forth their peddlers with verse and chapter of doom on their lips and a contract and pen in their hand.

Even an old gentleman in the Hefner community took out a policy. He was a farmer who worked a place in the bend of the river a couple of miles from the store. I barely remember this man, but when Dad mentioned the fellow's name it stirred the cogs and I could almost hear the high pitch of his voice. He took great pleasure in talking, and I always thought it was because his mother-in-law lived with his family. Maybe, he didn't talk a lot at home. Like so many of that time he had a nickname.

The farmer was having a hard time making ends meet, and when the insurance man came by, a light clicked in his head. He came rushing in the store, excited and telling of his good luck. "Jake," he said, "I bought one of those new life insurance policies on the ol' lady yesterday."

"That's good, Maize, anything happens to the wife, the kids will be pleased there's something there to bury their mother with."

"No, no, Jake! Not the ol' lady, her maw, Mrs. Babbit. If anything happens to her it's $250 right here." Maize patted the hip pocket of his overalls where his billfold rested.

"How old is Mrs. Babbit, now?" Dad asked.

"Ninety-two," Maize said. "Hell, I'm seventy-five and as bad as I feel, she can't last much longer."

A couple of years later Maize and his family came by. He said they were moving to town. They'd lost the place, and with just him and the "ol' lady" and Mrs. Babbit they'd just live in town. Maize hung back, and after the ladies had gone out to the car, he held a hand to his lips and spoke out of the side of his face. "Dang old woman's gonna live forever, Jake." He walked out, bent and wagging his head.

The advice offered was that leveraging securities was the smart way to go. Banks pushed debt by offering easy credit and low margins. It was a bad time to buy. Prohibition, the twenties, and then the Depression set the stage for Bonnie Parker and Clyde Barrow, bank robbing terrorist of Texas and the Midwest. Early in the next decade the stage curtains rose with a bang.

Crash Then Depression

Clyde Barrow liked fast Fords, heavy caliber automatic rifles, and banks with money. Henry's customers provided the cars, poorly guarded National Guard armories offered a source for the weapons, but in the early thirties banks with money were not that easily found. Still, Clyde Barrow was persistent.

In November 1934, sitting alone and despondent, a Missouri bank president likely considered his luck had reached bottom. A second later with the cold steel of Clyde's pistol pressing into his neck he realized that bottom was a relative term.

The young man holding the weapon hissed. "I want your money, all of it. Just put it in the sack."

"Son," said the banker. "They ain't none. This bank failed several weeks ago. We had a run. There's no money here."

Clyde discovered earlier that morning that an associate named Hardy had cheated him of $35 from a bank stickup the day before. The $80 they split three ways from that robbery had in fact been $115. Cheated and down to $28 net for two bank holdups he decided to head for Texas. Bankrupt banks were a liability even to robbers.

By 1928 most old enough to remember the financial "Panic of 1907" had chosen to forget its lessons. Perhaps the others thought something that bad could not happen a second time. "In November of 1907 the first National Bank of Mesquite, Texas, had announced a new policy. 'In keeping with actions of banks in Dallas and other surrounding communities, and owing to the fact that we cannot get any currency on the New York exchange, depositor's withdrawals will be limited to 5 percent of their balances in any one day, or 10 percent in any one week. Actual amounts will not exceed $20 in one day or $40 in one week.'"

In Haskell, the Piersons, father and sons, founded, worked in, and served as president of a bank for many years and at various times. So far as we know Bonnie and Clyde never tested it.

However, Sheriff Al Cousins did bring a robber into the bank one day. "I just want you to be able to identify this so-and-so in case he ever gets out of the penitentiary."

The sheriff explained, "He said he intended to hold up your bank but decided on a 'country bank' instead. Said he 'changed his mind here and became wary because the hardware store across the street sells guns.'"

The robber added, "You have a lot of women working here, too, and you can't tell what women will do."

Clyde Barrow apparently failed to share the Haskell robber's sentiments about the nervousness of women. His male partners changed rapidly, but the flamboyant Bonnie Parker seemed to be the only member of his gang pumping the same ice water that coursed through his veins.

After having assisted in several robberies, escapes from law enforcement officials, and kidnappings and/or murders, the newspapers labeled Bonnie as some kind of murderous, fast driving, fast living, cigar-smoking gun-moll. She mailed in a reply saying, "I don't smoke cigars."

In the cool predawn hours of January 16, 1934, she assisted Clyde when he and another partner stepped into the woods near Huntsville, Texas, to take on the Eastham Unit of the Huntsville Prison System in an attempted prison break for a fellow gang member.

With the aid of his Browning automatic rifle, virtually a machine gun, Clyde pulled off the caper but in so doing brought enough attention to himself to seal his fate. Within two weeks, Lee Simmons selected ex-Texas Ranger Frank Hamer as the man for the job of special agent with the task of running down Bonnie and Clyde. Hamer did so in less than six months.

Back in Haskell the bankers continued with self-pride in their frugality and conservatism. They worked hard to see that their bank served its customers properly. Alfred Pierson produced minutes of a bank meeting showing that his brother, "Marshall, once voluntarily went before the bank's board of directors and requested his salary be reduced from $35 a month to $30 a month. He told the board that he did not think the $35 justified."

No doubt, both bankers and financial institutions committed injustices at the time of the crash. But in general, this manmade disaster showed no mercy, destroying debtor and creditor alike.

"Jody Bender, who farmed land purchased by his great-grandfather along the south bank of Little Cypress, near Jefferson, said, 'It didn't take long to get used to the Depression. Cotton was cheap, corn went for thirty cents a bushel if you could sell it at all; you couldn't sell Irish potatoes.'

"Bender tried to trade his potatoes for oats at a wholesale grocery when oats were twenty-five cents a bushel. The grocer declined, saying, 'Oats will keep, but potatoes rot.'"

In the fall of 1999 I drank coffee with an eighty-one-year-old old-timer who asked for no break in life other than anonymity. He talked of the Depression and Dust Bowl days out along the Texas and New Mexico state line. He remembered his family putting their household belongings in the back of a truck and living out of it for months until the family had pulled enough cotton to pay off the last penny of their debt.

Ten years old when the banks collapsed, he said the despair caused by it and the subsequent dust storms were worse than ever recorded. His lips trembled as he related trauma controlled for seventy years. "Oh, the beginnings of the storms were often spectacular sights. Rolling clouds of sweeping sand would lift high into the sky in front of almost black clouds and then come roaring across the country. There was nothing pretty about the results, though.

"The crops were sandblasted and cut off at ground level. Soon the stock feed and grazing was gone and the coffee and flour and household groceries weren't far behind. We lived on bacon and eggs for a while—a strip of bacon one day and an egg the next." The man showed no sign of humor, his words stirred only sorrow.

"After the fences were covered or blown away, the topsoil removed and blown into dunes, there was nothing left for some but to start walking. People were literally found dead where they fell." The gentleman gathered himself. "This was near Hereford and the only thing good I got from it was teeth. I'm

Dust bowl.
Photo courtesy Texas State Library and Archives Commission

eighty-one and still have all my teeth except one wisdom tooth. They had a sign up there that said, 'not a cavity in town.'"

We stirred our coffee and I tried to think of some area of interest we might share. I hated to leave this man buried in dark memories. "Did you ever work on any of those wheat threshing crews?" I asked.

The first glimmer of a smile tugged at his lips. "I did, and you talk about eats! This one outfit had ladies that brought dinner each day in a station wagon. They would have the food already served out in individual containers. Dishpans was what they used, dishpans with a cup-towel covering them."

"And those big old straw stacks you guys produced there would look like mountains, huh? I remember the old cows would eat a tunnel into them in the winter."

My friend's face lit up. "They were a good place to take your best girl, too. They offered the only place in the county to get out of sight in some parts up there."

At about the time we spoke of, in his late teens and ready to prove his merit, Doyle Conine searched for work. Raised near Josephine he at one time headed west. Interestingly one of his trips took him toward Hereford. Like most other Americans, he walked, hitchhiked, and bummed freight rides, running down every rumor for employment that sounded valid. "That's the only way we had to get around," he said.

"Most of the freights I caught were at night. You could get a ride hitchhiking in the daytime, but people wouldn't much pick you up at night. Besides there were few cars on the roads at night."

"How's the best way to hop a freight?" I asked, delighted to at last find an authentic rider of the rails.

Doyle obviously sensed my enthusiasm. He had me reaching, but he was kind and let me down easy. "The best way is to find one sitting still," he laughed.

"I boarded one in Fort Worth once and rode to Big Springs, then caught another north toward Plainview. There were eight or twelve of us in that car going to Big Springs. The railroad men paid little attention. By then, people like us had swamped them."

"Did you find work?"

"Not much, I did help a man head maize, but it was too early for cotton picking. I made it back home after a couple of weeks. The weather cooperated on that trip. Open trains aren't much fun when it's cold."

The lure of the big engines affected Jack Spann also, but riding them wasn't enough. He wanted to drive them. After dusting the hay out of his hair and slapping the dust from his britches,

Jack Spann at Fort Sam Houston in San Antonio.

he got a job on the Frisco Rail line. His dream was fulfilled when they started student runs, and the regular fireman took a break in the doghouse, leaving him alone in the cab with the engineer.

"This engineer was an older man, a tough old coot, and I was pretty scared of him. Every other word from him was a cuss word, and he was breaking me in right. Well, the first thing at the beginning of a run you have to read your day orders. They give the instructions, tell you who else is on the line and everything important for a safe trip. Anytime you pull onto another company's line you have to get an order board for that line as well. Generally you hook those from a post, or stand, near the track without stopping. In smaller towns mail was picked up the same way. It was strung up there with a loop. You just stuck your arm through and hooked it as you whisked by."

It was easy to see this railroad time had marked high as a memorable event in Jack's eventful life. "Well on this student run we came off the Frisco line and down the hill this side of Sherman and onto the Southern Pacific line. The order board was strung on the left side of the track, coming south—my side.

"The engineer says, 'This one's yours, boy, hook it.'

"I'm leaning on the window, got my arm curved out there coming dead on at this loop when all of a sudden this old engine goes into one of those sideways wiggles, and I miss that darned thing." Jack chuckled.

"That old engineer grabbed the brake and sat back on it and cussed. 'Ought to make you walk back and get it,' he said. Getting that thing stopped and then that slow job of backing up was the longest train ride of my life."

Doyle had one more trip on his mind. "The wildest ride I ever had was in East Texas. I heard of a job in Kilgore and I had a cousin that hauled gas, 1,000 gallons at a time, between Gladewater and Royce City. I hitched a ride down there with him, but night caught me afoot, and I needed to get back. To make it worse it turned cold. Well I caught a train and was riding between cars standing and holding on a ladder.

"When that old boy got out of town and into the open, he lowered the ears on that thing. We were going along okay, and all of a sudden that train jerked and jumped, seemed like four or five feet. I was ready to get off the first chance I got. I remember spending the remainder of the night at a little old station down the track a ways. Cold and miserable, still, walking toward the light of that little old building felt good."

From Doyle's same community, but only five years old when the market crashed, Vivian Hess continued to see its impact on the country throughout her childhood. She recalled, "Grandfather Coffman raised show chickens. They were Rhode Island Reds and he showed them in Canada as well as the States and South America. Unbelievably, he sold eggs from his best lines for a dollar apiece and this was in the middle of the Depression, mind you. People bought them for hen settings."

Mrs. Gilbert Hess (Vivian)

Farther west in Knox County and newly married when the crash hit, J. T. Murdock, like others his age had little to lose to economic trends. The first year of their lives together, he and mother lived in a dirt-floored smokehouse. The smokehouse was part of the deal for lowered day wages as a farmhand that were never paid in full. Still, they had a roof over their heads. In 1930 unlike some, Dad had a second job.

Prentiss McNeil owned the gin and the gin had yards full of 500-pound bales of cotton. Finding someone who could balance atop a bale of cotton resting flat on a truck-bed and, with a hook in each hand, lift and wrestle another bale into position was difficult. From three to four men worked on the ground lifting the bale. Blessed with strength, Dad filled the high spot need.

Loading baled cotton in 1931, J. T. "Jake" Murdock on top.

He remembered, "The gin ran strong through Christmas that year. On New Year's Eve, Mac shut her down to allow the crew a night off for the holiday season. He handed each hand his pay and asked, 'Anybody want a job tonight as night watchman?'"

Mom said her little sister, Aunt Goldia, joined them at the scale-house for New Year's Eve. With a coal-fed fire, a basket lunch, and an electric light shining out the window of the small scale-house they welcomed New Year.

Norris Curtis recalled loading Hunt County cotton at about that time. "We'd load those bales from the ground to the bed of those Model-A Fords. There'd be bales of cotton all over them gin yards. Us young guys could always get a job that time of year loading trucks. Wages were about fifteen cents an hour but we got thirty-five cents each for loading a truck. They hauled thirteen bales at a time. Took 'em to Houston."

"Like everything else at that time those old gins were dangerous places to work," Doyle Conine said. "We had a man get hung up in those saws and nearly lose an arm. You see that cotton fell down those stands and those saws were back in under there. Well, they were always getting stopped up, and this man took a stick and was lying on his back poking at that cotton in the saws trying to free it.

"He said something told him to get a hold with his free hand, and he grabbed a rail and about that time the jam came free. It was wire that had got in that cotton someway. It wrapped around his stick then his arm, and then those teeth on the saws and that wire just kept pulling his arm in farther and farther. He was stretched out there on his back when they got it shut off. Having a hold with that other hand saved him. He didn't even lose the arm, but it was a ribbon of scars where those teeth sawed at it."

The bad times continued with declining values crushing those in debt and those providing the credit. The noose of deflation and lost income strangled the more established Texans. Like J. T. Murdock, Bedi Taylor's situation was different. He realized a dream. Young, married, and clerking in Riordan's Hardware Store in Colorado City, he was making wages wearing a white shirt and miles from the nearest mule. He liked the store business and had taken a radio course down at Austin.

The down side of all this was the Depression sapping the resources of the county. The people were suffering for money, but Mr. Taylor figured it hard to lose something you'd never had. Thirty-five years later he recalled witnessing a sign of the times he'd almost forgotten.

In the summer of 1931, eager for a sale and standing near the storefront, Bedi smiled as a farmer walked in, removed a sweat-stained hat, and looked around. "Boy, where's Mr. Riordan?"

Bedi pointed.

The farmer walked to the back of the store where the owner sat at his desk. "Jerald, we need to talk about that Maytag."

Mr. Riordan pulled up a chair for the man and Bedi edged closer. He overheard the farmer complain about cheap farm prices, the poor droughty crop, and sick children. The farmer concluded with the fact that there was no way he could pay Mr. Riordan the $21.25 he owed on the washing machine. Even the $2.50 a month payment was impossible. He asked permission to load it up and return it the following Saturday.

Mr. Riordan looked with drawn face past counters piled with merchandise, through the display window, and into the dusty street. "Sam, times are hard, indeed. Yesterday young Taylor and I took in $1.75. All day, a $1.75! I got no use for a used washing machine. Don't you have anything out there you might convert to cash."

The farmer looked for a place to spit then bull's-eyed the spittoon. "Gotta keep my team. They ain't nothing else out there we don't eat from." He stood, shook his head then turned to go. He stopped. "Would you take a paper?"

"What kind of paper?"

"A drummer stopped by two or three years ago, before the crash. We'd just sold our cotton. Anyway, I bought this Franklin Life Insurance paper from him. It says stock certificate. I paid $50 dollars for it. You want it for the washer?"

"Bring it in, Sam. If it looks okay, we'll call her even."

Halfway to the door, the farmer looked up, stopped, and turned. His face carried a sheepish expression. "One thing, Jerald, last week's market for that paper was $1.25, best I could tell."

"Bring it on. If it checks out, something is better than nothing for both of us."

I thought of Mr. Riordan that day as I watched Bedi finish his story and glance out the window into that same street. It was paved now, but still dust swirled. I knew Bedi acted as executor for his old partner's estate and, more recently, for that of Mrs. Riordan.

"When we probated the will, a few weeks ago, those certificates amounted to something like $27,000 for the heirs."

Earlier, Prohibition failed to erase the habit of drinking. Ten years later the market's crash encouraged many financially broken men to lean on the bottle. Suicide, nervous breakdown, and loss of self-esteem were symptomatic of the change that tormented thousands.

The perception the business world and other citizens held of banks and financial institutions changed for many. Some never trusted the institutions again regardless of government oversight. Most came back to the deposit window after a few years.

Before the wild years of the twenties, Texas's earlier businessmen were thrifty and some even held a reputation for parsimony. After the Depression those views were strengthened for many. One of the richest, Colonel W. L. Moody of Galveston, is said to have positioned his desk by the office door to enable him to check the clock as his employees came to work. In 1908 applicants for employment in his firm were asked to recite the Lord's Prayer, spell Tuesday, and explain one-eighth and one thirty-second of a dollar.

Perhaps the Depression influenced his son, W. L. Moody (2nd), who wrote his philosophy of business for his grandson in 1945. "Be truthful, fair in dealings, do not take advantage of your fellow man; do not gamble, especially in the stock market; do not smoke or drink. They are vulgar and expensive habits that lead you nowhere."

Records indicate W. L. Moody (2nd) may have found his son lacking in business principals. According to *Galveston: A History*, W. L. Moody (2nd) died in 1954 and left $1 to his son, W. L. Moody (3rd), a foundation estimated at $440 million to various state welfare organizations, and his business empire to his daughter, Mary Moody Northern."

Harris Kempner, early partner and longtime associate of the Moodys, later became estranged from his old partner's family and delighted in taking "digs" in their direction. He claimed, "The Colonel's wife owns a car but doesn't like to drive it because she has to buy gasoline. It's a cruel dilemma for her, however, because not driving the vehicle allows the tires to rot."

In 1933 most Texans were totally unaware of either the Moodys or the Kimpners. Their counties had just begun receiving federal help to alleviate economic misery. Van Zandt County was typical of those across the state, and their writers state, "In January 1933, the Reconstruction Finance Corporation granted $10,000 for several county projects, including the repair of water mains and planting of trees along highways.

"The Civil Works Administration (C.W.A.) provided a nurse and $6,150 for malarial drainage. In May 1933, fifteen young men left for Civilian Conservation Corps (C.C.C.) camps. With money supplied by the Public Works Administration (P.W.A.), county officials erected and furnished a 'debt-free' courthouse and jail."

And then the biggest federal program of all came in October 1935, the Works Progress Administration (W.P.A.). Streets and roads were paved, parks were established, and across the state, embarrassed but thankful men went to work, uncomfortable at being on the federal payroll but thankful for a job. These men took their "ribbing" from comments like, "It takes four WPA men to do one man's job—one to work, one going to the water bucket, one coming from the bucket, and the fourth guarding the bucket." Most ultimately agreed the programs helped pull a nation out of a bad time.

Harris Kempner apparently had little use for the government's involvement in the nation's economy. His following comment suggests he also experienced some of the ups and downs of parenthood while patriarch of his own dynastic family. Speaking of his son, Isaac H. Kempner, he said, "If at twenty you are not socialistic, you have no heart. If at forty you are still socialistic, you have no mind."

"I don't know," Dad said, "You start talking about Roosevelt and the New Deal and the first thing you know you're into politics. People say, Republican this, Democrat that. Look what we did, look what they didn't do. The thing is, at that time something had to be done. The country was about to go into a revolution, and little kids were hurting.

"We lost some freedom, but some wrongs were righted, too. But, I'll tell you, what was hard to make sense of was when they sent teams around to buy cattle and then shoot them. Now, that was hard to understand. And people hungry in every city in the country." Dad shook his head in disbelief of what his own eyes had witnessed.

"That really happened?"

"It sure did," he said. "Vernor had several yearlings. I think they paid him, I believe it was $7 for yearlings and about $17.50 for a cow. Then they shot them."

With years of caring for stock in their blood, shooting them made little sense to a Texian. But, these folks who brought us off the frontier and through the Depression were tough, resilient, and hard as hickory knots. Still, like their descendents they were vulnerable. When reality became too terrible to contemplate, like Scarlet O'Hara, they sometime denied it, set it aside for tomorrow.

Lester Bowman grew up during those early years of the century. He raised good wheat crops and cattle along the Knox and Haskell County lines. His fence bordered the road across from one of Dad's. They shared work, laughs, and life. Small, tough, and a good neighbor, Lester drove over to see about Dad when he missed him for a few days.

Dad had been sick, and the doctors had him taking it easy while tests were being run. Lester drove his pickup into the yard and honked. Dad walked out and greeted him.

Bowman pushed his straw hat back and folded his arms on the window of his pickup. "Been hot, ain't it?"

Dad wiped his forehead and nodded. He leaned against the pickup and scraped toe designs in the dust.

"Missed you a few days. Anything wrong?"

"Wal, yeah, Lester, the doctors are running some tests. Told me to stay off that tractor a few days."

Lester's concern showed. "What they looking at?"

"Heart." Dad admitted.

"My God, Jake! Times is too hard for heart trouble."

Regardless of how bad times became, neither socialism nor its big brother communism took over the nation. Still, they may have been closer than thought by many. Texas, more agricultural and less industrialized than the Northeast, was spared much of the conflict involved in the labor movement in that area. With their distrust of bankers, lawyers, and politicians, and with only a small number of traditions older than a few generations of good saddle horses, its citizens busied themselves embracing the changing times brought about by the gasoline engine.

Trucking
When Dumb
Was Good

In the days before local auction barns provided country markets, Texas communities had scattered livestock traders. In the Knox County area in the 1930s, the Ratliff brothers earned their keep plying this trade. A farming area, many families owned livestock, and these traders loved to find the animals new homes.

Behind the barns small pastures carried a half dozen or so beef cattle, a milk-cow, and either horse or mule teams. In addition hogs were raised and butchered at home. Since sows were prolific there were always a few hogs around for sale.

Farmers knew crops, teams, and other livestock in that order. Cowboys studied animals' temperament, motivation, and habits, paying little attention to their value. Farmers watched livestock markets closer, and ranchers kept an even keener eye on price. Still, the cattle traders knew the markets best. They honed their trading skills and had little interest in weight gain or animal reproduction.

The larger ranches, after railroads networked the country, shipped most of their cattle by train. Even then, it was not unusual for cattle traders to buy special lots of groups too small or too far from the track to fill a freight car. By the mid-thirties this need developed into a new industry. Trucking or cattle hauling came of age in Texas. Some said this new crossbreed, sort of a hybrid between the cowboy, the rancher, the farmer, and the trader, didn't have to know anything. Some thought a lack of knowledge an asset in truckers.

In the early thirties, having acquired a Ford truck and a good working relationship with Raymond and Will Ratliff, J. T. Murdock found himself busy as a tumblebug in a mule barn. What the two brothers bought, he hauled. He quickly learned this new profession that said all one needed was a good truck and a blank mind.

Dad said, "Raymond had me deliver a load of cattle out to old man Ern Lowe once. I hadn't been hauling for the Ratliffs too long, but Mr. Lowe and I had met. By the time I got backed up to the lot gate and we exchanged a few words, I could tell the old man was a little fidgety. As soon as we got through wondering if it would ever rain again, he started quizzing me. I guess he was afraid he'd been snookered on the deal.

"He started off with 'Jake, what did the Ratliffs pay for these cows?'

"I don't know, Mr. Lowe. You want to leave that gate open over yonder or close it?"

"'Oh, shut the dern thing I guess. Murdock, where'd the boys buy this stock?'

"I just shook my head and went about my business, pulling the end-board gate up to unload the bunch.

"'What you reckon this bunch will weigh, Merdick?' The old man asked, twisting my name a little just to nudge me.

"Pretty heavy, Mr. Lowe, they're good stock."

"'Son, you reckon these cows are springing or are ready for a bull.'

"I wouldn't have any idea, sir." I shut the gate as the last one jumped out. I tightened the chain on the end gate and walked toward the cab. "Been good talking to you, Mr. Lowe. See you 'fore long." I realized then, he'd followed me to the truck.

"He folded both arms on the door's open window, turned his head and spit, then looked me in the eye. 'Murdock,' he said, 'you're the best damn trucker I ever saw. You don't know nothing.' He smiled—just barely."

Murdock not only hauled from the Ratliff's pens in Goree, Texas, to the Fort Worth stockyards, but he frequently made the buying rounds with one of the brothers.

Ivy League business schools have tried to capture the essence of business fundamentals for generations. Their efforts certainly demand respect; however, it may well be that these old-time traders dispensed more business know-how in a minute than Harvard offers in a semester.

Most small stockmen and farmers were glad to see traders pull off the dusty road and into their drive. They knew he planned to "skin" them if he could, but if the man had a good reputation and a friendly nature, time with him beat spending it away from a crop trying to locate a market for only a few animals. Besides country life was lonesome, and traders knew the gossip. All the same, every transaction was a contest and no one wanted to be bested.

"Raymond had me turn in at this farmer's place," Dad remembered. "Ratliff had spotted the old fellow out at the lot. He'd already told me he had been trying to buy this particular cow.

"They dickered around awhile, looking at the cow in question as she stood there in the lot. Raymond admired the cow's good qualities then seemed saddened and expressed regret that age had begun to work on her a little. He mentioned how long he'd been seeking a cow like that and reckoned her being aged just a little had settled her down enough to make her a good keeper. He ended with, 'Yes sir, I wish I had that cow, I'd keep that cow and raise one of those good babies every year.'

"Finally the two reached a deal and the farmer sold Raymond the cow. Ratliff paid the man, and I backed the truck up to where the wheels dropped down into a low place near his gate. We made sort of a makeshift chute out of the barn on one side and the gate on the other.

"Before we loaded the cow the man said, 'Come around here, Ratliff, and look at these three shoats.'

"'Have they got ears and tails?' Raymond asked.

"'Got what?' the old man asked.

"'Ears and tails,' Raymond said. 'I'll give $.50 a head more for a shoat that's got a good stout tail and a full ear on him. I never saw a shoat me and Murdock couldn't load if he had a good hand hold.'"

Piglet's tails and ears are subject to freezing in cold weather. They were also often deliberately cut off for marking purposes in those days. With high truck beds and flimsy chutes and lots, a handhold on a fighting shoat was a consideration.

I could tell Dad worked to hold back a grin, so I knew there was an end to this story I'd yet to hear. "Raymond was unable to buy the three shoats. We loaded the cow, and as we drove back onto the road and out of earshot he sighed and allowed the grin to spread across his face. 'Yeah, Jake, I'll keep that booger just as long as it takes for you to get her to Fort Worth.'"

Henry Ford came out with the V-8 in 1933. Dad realized weight and rolling tires meant the difference in profitability and idle sightseeing. The trucking business required power, and soon he traded for a V-8. Now, he could haul bigger loads. In cattle that meant if the animals were big stuff, grown cows or bulls, about six.

Soon afterwards he began to see a few rigs around the Fort Worth docks that had trailers attached between the cab and in front of the rear tires by means of a pin similar to a wagon's kingpin. Instead of a bed fixed solidly to the truck's frame, these trailers, with their additional set of rear dual wheels, permitted a much larger cargo space. A few trips later Dad had fashioned a homemade trailer to replace his flatbed and was hauling even heavier loads.

This may have been the first semi-trailer-truck rig to routinely operate west of Fort Worth in the North Central Texas region. It seems a miracle his story was of success instead of tragedy for he had no trailer brakes, no heater, and used a lit candle for a windshield defroster during icy conditions. Even those roads that were paved were narrow, humpbacked, cut-shouldered affairs that became slick with the slightest moisture. Add all this to the fact that a live load that is constantly shifting and bouncing a truck around is arguable the most difficult cargo imaginable, and one gets an idea of the odds faced by those drivers.

"I was traveling in high-cotton by the time I got that first V-8," Dad said. "I could make it round trip in about sixteen-seventeen hours if I had no trouble getting them loaded. I remember making twenty-nine trips one January."

I shook my head remembering from childhood the expression on Mom's face the day she noticed the several hundred yards of telephone wire strung behind that old rig while Dad snored, jumped, and jerked in bed trying to catch a short nap.

"I got Lloyd to go with me on that last trip, though, so I could sleep a little," Dad said.

I sensed Dad's memory carried him seventy years back in time. He'd become animated, seeming to squint at the pale glow of 6-volt headlights timidly nudging the finite wall of darkness that swallowed light and narrow pavements. "That old ridge-back stretch of blacktop between Jacksboro and Azel could get the slickest of anything I ever saw. Even a dew could turn that thing into a skating rink."

He chuckled. "Remember one time, about three in the morning, I was loaded heavy going in. I wasn't doing but about 25 and I'd been following these lights ahead of me up and down those hills for about twenty minutes. I had it in third gear most of the time, groaning up those old hills and then easing down them. Every once in a while, I'd see those lights up ahead there whip sideways and wiggle around some, and I knew that man was having trouble on that slick road.

"All of a sudden those lights whipped around and did a full circle. One second they pointed toward Fort Worth, then the next instant they flashed right into my eyes and on around and back toward the east. Well, the fellow brought that little roadster to a halt right in the middle of the road. I pulled up beside him real slow.

"When I got even he just sat there, both hands straight in front with a rigid grip on either side of that steering wheel. 'Sir,' I said, 'Do you need any help?'

"The man turned to me, and even in that moonlight you could see the paleness of his face.

"'No,' he said, 'except, which way is Fort Worth?' Dad laughed and cleaned his glasses. 'That poor man had no idea which way he was headed.'"

Dr. Arnecke, who practiced in Dewitt County, avoided the dilemma of whether to give priority to his patients or to take time away from them and learn to drive. At sixty years of age, progress dictated that the days of a doctor muddling along dirt roads in a buggy were too slow and outdated. He is said to have bought a new 1920 custom Model-T and then hire two drivers. He never learned to drive.

It is difficult to remember that in the twenties and thirties most highways in Texas were gravel or nonexistent. The road to Lubbock from Fort Worth was unpaved through the Cap Rock area and so was Ranger Hill on Interstate 20.

Before settling into double harness, Bedi Taylor challenged the 270 miles to Fort Worth from Loraine a number of times. It seems he'd met a young lady on the trolley in Fort Worth who made gravel roads and flat tires secondary. Long and steep Ranger Hill was on his route.

"Driving to Fort Worth then was sorta like that road on TV," Bedi said. "You know what I mean, out there, by California, in Mexico."

"You mean 'Running the Baja?'" I asked.

"Yeah, that's it. That's what I think of when I see that thing. You know them old cars back then had the gas tanks mounted high. They were all gravity fed. If the tank got about half empty and you were going up, why the gas wouldn't flow."

Visions of terrible deaths and modern lawsuits filled my head. "Some gas tanks were in front of the passengers, weren't they?"

"That's right and others you had to raise the passenger seat to fill the tank. Well, when I'd come to Ranger Hill, coming home, I'd have to turn around and back up it so the engine wouldn't die. Take forever to just get up that hill."

Mr. Taylor thought of all this for a moment while working the ash from his cigar with his little finger. "I remember when Kurt set the record from Fort Worth to Loraine."

"How long did it take him?"

"No, it wasn't the speed record. He was the first one to ever drive it all the way without a flat."

Paul Carter made his living working with his hands, first as an aviation mechanic during World War II then later as a cabinetmaker and carpenter. Born in 1921, he remembers early cars. "Our first car was a two-seat, T-model ragtop. It had a little lever or handle at the top of the windshield that could be manually turned back and forth to make the wipers move. If I'm not mistaken that car had a dummy door on the driver's side and you had to enter through the front passenger door. Our first glass enclosed car was a Whippet."

Jack Spann added, "Willis came out with an early car that was a real beauty. I think they called it the Willis Knight. It had wooden spoke wheels, but I guess the Graham Page took the cake for the fanciest."

Those travelers in the thirties who dirtied windshields going toward Lubbock from Fort Worth had a friend in a fellow named Carl Hash. Mr. Hash ran a service station and restaurant and catered to truckers. His place sat on top of a hill so you were already slowed down when you got there, and you could pick up speed in any direction when leaving.

Practical men tend to do well in business, and Carl had a good thing going until things, out of his control, began to go wrong. It's hard to tell if good times or bad times bring out the worst in human nature, but the thirties were hard times, and many didn't mind crossing over the law to keep a little green in their pocket. As a matter of fact, the law themselves, at times, could not find the line. Such a situation developed near Hash's station. Forty-five years after the occurrence Dad came back from a fishing trip and told me the story.

"Saw a man down at the lake last week that remembered when that constable, or night-watchman, or whatever he was, hitched up with that state trooper and near put old Hash out of business back in the thirties."

"I guess I don't know this story," I said.

Dad ran an eye over me, like he wondered where I'd been, and continued. "Yeah, they stopped me one night. It was this little old wide spot, just this side of Hash's, about five miles. This constable and a state trooper had them a sweet little deal going down there. I knew about it. I'd talked to some of the boys they'd already got. Well, it was not long after Don L. and I rigged up my trailer. I was loaded heavy going towards the stockyards. Course I was overweight, everybody ran that way. You had to."

"Who controlled that, the Railroad Commission?" I asked.

"Yeah, course, you can guess how friendly the railroad was to truckers."

"What'd they say?"

"They were in the trooper's car. The constable sitting in the passenger's seat. They told me to drive over to some little old lots they had there and unload the cattle. They were going to weigh the rig. Looks of my papers, they thought I was overweight. I asked if there was water in those lots.

"This constable said, 'no.'

"'I ain't putting this man's cattle in no dry lot,' I says. At this point that constable starts acting like he's going to do me a big favor.

"'Well you can just pay the fine and go on then,' he said.

"'How much?'

"'Twenty dollars,' the constable says.

"I reach for the glove box. 'I'll give you a check.'

"'No, you don't understand. It's got to be cash.' They both piped up about the same time.

"Well, I offered to go up to Hash's and convert a check to cash, but they'd have none of that. Finally, I guess they decided it was either shoot me, let me go, or follow me up to Hash's, so they agreed to follow me and wait outside while I went in. I knew I was being ripped off, but what could I do?

"When I got there I parked out front and they parked beside me and motioned me in. They didn't budge.

"I asked Hash if I could write him a check, and he said sure then took a look at me and said, 'Jake what's going on?'

"I told him.

"'You hungry?' he asked. I thought he was picking a strange time to sell a hamburger. Well he started explaining how those guys were so bad they were ruining his business. Truckers were taking other roads to bypass the trap, and he was about to go under. He said he'd already had words with both men.

"'Jake you go take a seat back there at that table against the wall. I'll fix you a T-bone. If you want, after you've eaten I'll let you have the twenty if you still want it.'

"'What if they come in here after me?' I ask.

"'They won't come in here, Murdock. They know what I've got under this counter and what will happen if they step through that door. I've told them. No, they won't come in here.'"

Dad let the silence stretch.

"So..." I said.

"I finished my steak, went outside, and they'd given up and left. It wasn't long after that the state cleaned them out."

Carl Nicholson remembered driving trouble of a different kind, but a little less threatening. "Earlier I'd driven a Model-A then Chevrolets, then in 1936 Lorine and I bought a 1932

Hupmobile Sport Coupe for $150. It had a powerful straight-eight motor, two spare tires, set-in wells in the front fenders, and in the style of the times, an upholstered rumble seat. I bought it because it was in good shape and cheap. Later I learned the factory had shut down and spare parts were no longer easily available. It used odd-size tires.

Ragtop traffic.

"In those days flats were common, and most people carried repair kits and hand-tire pumps as well as spare tires. On a trip between Athens and Port Lavaca, a flat caught me unprepared. I had no spare nor did I have a repair kit. Fortunately, I had a jack and a lug wrench so was able to remove the tire and by hitchhiking to and from town with my tire for a companion was soon able to get us underway again."

Lora Murdock remembered the early days of automobiles in Knox and Baylor Counties. "When we got our first car, something was always going wrong with it. Before long Poppa became a good mechanic. We'd all get in the car to go to

Bomarton, and that old car would sputter and die. Poppa would get out and raise one side of the hood and tinker around a minute. Then he'd ask, 'You got a hairpin, Dovey?'

"Mamma would give him a hairpin and soon we'd be on our way. After a year or so Poppa quit farming and opened a garage and filling station in Bomarton."

"I had a great-aunt that lived in Melissa." Doyle Conine said. "She had an automobile that was air cooled. It was a Franklin. That thing impressed me. It stuck in my head. I couldn't get used to the idea of no radiator."

By the latter part of the 1930s, automobiles had made the buggy obsolete. Local livestock barns were changing the nature of the small independent cattle-trader and putting him in front of an auctioneer or on the management end of his own sale barn. The horse and mule trader, however, felt the cold wind of change with the coming of the tractor only a couple of years before the end of the decade. When change came to them, it came swiftly.

Whoa! Tractor

If they weren't working they didn't eat. They didn't know "whoa" from "giddy-up," but they could kick as hard as a mule. In the 1930s gasoline-powered tractors swept across the farm belt as a replacement to teams. They brought a new curse word—"crank." There is little doubt that farmers received as many broken arms in the first years of using tractors as they previously suffered at the feet of their kicking animals.

Like their automobile counterparts, the first tractors came without starters. If you were lucky, they were equipped with a crank having two ninety degree angles that allowed you to "turn over" the motor manually. Upon achieving ignition, too frequently a bruised forearm resulted from the thing slapping the user.

Those not so lucky chose a "popping-Johnny" tractor that used a flywheel instead of a crank for a starter. These tractors' nickname was a melding of their manufacturer's name, John Deere, and a description of their engine's sound. Seeing less fortunate neighbors go by with broken arms, these popping-Johnny owners found their own joy short-lived. Their ranks rapidly thinned.

Word got around that the flywheel Johnnies had the bad habit of starting while the new owner absentmindedly had left it in gear. Since the owner had to be standing on the ground to crank or turn a flywheel, many of the new mechanized farmers were losing the race with their heavier equipment and going into permanent retirement.

Doyle Conine mentioned, "As soon as manufacturers solved the problem of cranking, the Ferguson Company came out with a state-of-the-art machine that threatened to capture the light tractor market. Quiet, powerful, and with an electric starter, this little Ford of the fields had only one problem. When connected to a heavy load, its front had a tendency to rear up, then the whole thing was subject to falling over backward. By changing the pull point for the draw bar, this was eventually corrected."

Doyle continued, "Not only were the tractors dangerous, but so was the equipment. A fellow over in Collin County was using a shredder one day that had a nail in the drive shaft for a pin. He was by himself and stopped out in the field and got off with the machine idling and the drive shaft running. The shaft caught in his clothing and pulled him down to the ground. Those blades hit his head and killed him. When they found him, the only clothing on him was one shirt sleeve, Most of what this country has learned about safety, they come by it hard."

More discouraging than the danger of the new machines was their endurance. They never tired.

Breathing a team offered an excuse to roll a smoke, get a drink of water, perhaps even catch a moment's shut-eye after dinner. With the advent of the tractor that all changed. Now the poor farmer, stripped of his façade of invincibility, had to stand before his helpmate and admit, "It's me, not the dern machine that's tired."

The conversion from teams to tractors occurred at a rapid rate. Throughout the blackland and on up the rolling plains the industry committed to supplying horses and mules crashed similarly to the earlier stock market. Owners of good, stout, matched teams that would bring $500 to $1,000 in 1929 were lucky to find buyers willing to pay $150 for the same team a decade later.

The horse and mule trader was swept aside by the tractor and implement man and left to a battle of the fittest for the dwindling draft animal market. Only the shrewdest trader could find a home for these animals that had so many years been a part of man's existence. Large animals continued to be used in the muddy oil fields of East Texas, and smaller mules filled a limited need in mines. A few teams continued to be used for another decade in eastern sections of the state, on smaller acreage farms.

As most were saying good-bye to their horses and mules, Eugene Jones claims to have been saying hello. Jones entered the army as an eighteen-year-old in 1938. "I was assigned to Fort Clark, the 5th U.S. Army Horse Cavalry. When we got down there, they issued me a uniform.

"I got my clothes and moved on to a table where this sergeant says, 'You ever ride a horse, Son?'

"No Sir."

"'Well good! We got one out there ain't never been rode. You two ought to fit pretty good.'"

Jones was one of the last young men to fall for the old sergeant's line. Within a few months the army also mechanized and said good-bye to their mounts. No state had a more dependent relationship with draft animals than did Texas. A small niche remained for the working cow-horse but the large horse, the mule, and the oxen were soon to become only a memory.

One of these places the working cowpony managed to continue earning its keep was in the range lands around King County. Parks Norris managed and held the job of foreman on a ranch, the Ross Circle O, near there. For the Norris family this was the culmination of a dream. Parks had been sidetracked, herding water leaks in the small country town of Goree while his wife taught school for a number of years.

Their son, Jimmy, had a job on the ranch as cowboy, and Mrs. Norris was employed to cook and manage the ranch house for these two plus two extra hands. Jimmy and I had been classmates until we finally conned our way into the adult world shortly before the end of the forties. I visited with them shortly after they took on these new responsibilities. The spread was not a large operation, but it remained about as unchanged from a hundred years earlier as things could be.

The Circle O outfit encloses mostly rough country, and this bunch of punchers looked like walking wounded. One of the other men answered to Sheep. He'd failed to get a finger out of the way when he took a dally around his saddle horn a few days earlier while roping. I think the doctors may have saved the finger, but he wasn't very handy for a few days.

As best I could tell, what was going on there was that Sheep and the other puncher, both around thirty and top hands, had built a reputation working for the big ranches, and they wanted to impress their new boss.

Parks and Jimmy on the other hand, as salty as they come but still a little rusty from all those years over in the row-crop side of the county, were pressing hard to carry their own weight. Jimmy teased his dad about forgetting the collar rig his lariat threaded through when he attempted to run past and throw a roped cow shortly after Sheep got banged up. Perhaps it was Sheep's problem with the dally that prompted Parks to tie fast, in any case, cow, rope, and saddle stayed with the somersaulting horse, but the foreman parted with all.

I managed one of those good ranch meals there and offered to help Mrs. Norris with the dishes. This lady had known me all my life, but somehow I still had her fooled. Well, maybe I didn't have her fooled totally. As I remember, she washed and I dried. Still, she wanted to talk and acted glad to have company. She laughingly told me of Sheep's first offer to help with dishes and his explanation of his skills in that area.

"Ol' Sheep got the suds stirred up good and said, 'Mrs. Norris I ain't the hastiest and the tastiest, but shore, I'm the fastest and the nastiest.'"

Much has been written about the cowboy and his mount's performance at places like the Circle O, but few would argue that a good draft animal was less trained or cared for. The teamster, whether a farmer or a freighter, knew his animals and they knew him. Together they were a symphony of energy performing feats of labor beyond the imagination. When gathering crops of corn or milo maize, voice commands of men working a significant distance away from the wagon and team directed the animal's movement. In fields of young plants, an experienced animal walked, contrary to natural tendencies, on the difficult footing of the high beds, away from the tender sprouts. Rigs of enormous size and weight were backed, turned, and maneuvered into difficult places. Trained to high levels, huge animals, working from the smallest cue, stepped sideways in unison, almost tiptoeing like a ballerina.

More than one adult face turned to avoid seeing the implement man drive his "boot," taken as trade-in, away from the old home place. Many of these families knew the background of their teams better than their own. No doubt, a few were prouder of that heritage.

Mule team of 30 plus animals.
Photo courtesy Texas State Library and Archives Commission

As a young girl of twelve, Mary (Banks) Pruitt moved from Georgia to Texas around 1900. She reported a family story that reveals that at least one notorious lady of the nineteenth century would go to amazing lengths to improve the lineage of her animals.

Speaking of her husband, Mrs. Pruitt said, "Henry was raised near St. Paul, Minnesota. That is where the famous James boys, Frank and Jesse, and Belle Starr lived for a while. Henry's dad had an experience with Belle Starr that we all found enchanting. Will had a thoroughbred horse and one day when he was riding, Bell Starr met him on the road and, knowing good horses, she demanded that he let his horse breed with her mare.

"Naturally, being a gentleman of the 'old country' he refused because he felt this was not something a lady should observe in the presence of a man. She drew her gun and made him dismount and let the horses breed while she held the gun on him."

The evolution away from the horse and to more efficient means of production could be as easily overdramatized as it could be underemphasized. To each generation born prior to the Great Depression, the beasts of burdens were a significant and integral part of most lives. However, these are the same people who pioneered the development of air travel, modern medicine, radio, the telephone, electricity, and the atomic age. While doing all that, they prepped the rest of us for a cold war, semiconductors, the space era, and ultimately the information age. They were not lightweights, and above all they did not let old ways influence new brilliance. They were the doers, the builders, the shakers, and the enemies of the status quo.

Radios, Ice, and Smokeless Lamps

By 1939 the mule had left the farm, cars were at nearly every house, telephones served towns located on highways, and holes for giant wooden poles were being dug along country roads to bring the modern marvel of electricity to the most remote homes.

Challenged by competition from automobiles, both truck and car, the railroads pushed spur rail lines to smaller towns and markets across the state. The area of deep clay and heavy rainfall around Dallas offered a challenge to this roadbed construction.

Vivian Hess, as a child in Josephine, watched railroad construction engineers make do with what raw material they had. She said, "When they built the rail line through Josephine, Nevada, and on beyond, they baked that black ground into a red gravel-like material to use for a roadbed."

I perked up. I'd never heard of this. "Yes," she said, "They dug a tunnel nearly a quarter mile long and filled it with firewood and then burned that for weeks. Later they dredged up that dirt surrounding those tunnels and the black clay had turned red and was more like gravel than anything else. That's what they used on that whole roadbed."

A few years earlier and a short distance south, on this same blackland east of Dallas, Walter Allen and his brother-in-law

Robert L. Warren had exposed the citizens and, more importantly, their carriage animals to the frightening experience of the first automobile in Terrell, Texas. Their weekly jaunts created numerous runaways and much confusion. Reports say Walter had sort of an innovative nature, but it sounds like Robert may have just been a good brother-in-law, participating in the joint partnership for the sake of family interest. Their phones were said to ring constantly on Sunday with people wanting to know what time the family would be taking the machine out.

Even earlier, Abilene and Ballinger were served with telephone lines that passed through Buffalo Gap riding piggyback on a barbed-wire fence. Some complained about the quality of reception. The service was said to improve in 1910 when the exchange went into a two-story house.

This was the year that Captain R. C. Lyons sold the new hotel he'd built in Buffalo Gap to his daughter and son-in-law, Mr. and Mrs. John Kincaid. According to the *Taylor County History*, "Hotel rooms (called apartments) were furnished with the old-fashioned high-post bedsteads and shuck mattresses. The beds were covered with a woven counterpane. There was a small bureau with a washbowl and pitcher in each room and a kerosene lamp. The floors were bare, and there was no heat in the building except for the stove in the downstairs hall."

It seems the gap made famous by buffaloes wasn't the only West Texas area to find a dual purpose for the new barbed wire. Clem "Doc" Reynolds lived through the early years in Randall County. He mentioned the crank-phone period. "We had a barbed-wire telephone. One Sunday Mother and Dad went to visit one of the neighbors. About the middle of the afternoon the phone rang and one of the boys answered.

"Mother said, 'Are you boys smoking over there?'"

"No, ma'am."

"'Well, I was sure I could smell smoke over this phone.'"

Doc said, "We hurrahed her about that as long as she lived."

Mrs. Henry Pruitt remembered home delivery as the latest convenience a decade earlier in Humble. "Our ice was delivered daily with a horse and wagon, driven by Harold Sheffield, a high school boy. Once a week we looked forward to the vegetable wagon, which was driven by 'Old Pete' from whom we bought fresh vegetables. Life was different then. If we wanted to see a movie, we had to walk a mile to catch the jitney and go to Humble and see silent movies."

Vivian Hess of Garland also remembered the days of home delivery. "There were large cardboard signs with different weights of ice you could buy. You could just leave that sign inside the screen and that's what the iceman would leave."

Reverend Hines' country home had no electricity. "We did get a radio that ran on a battery, though. The first radios used battery power. Later some folks had wind-chargers to charge the batteries. We also had a gramophone. You know, the kind you wound up by hand with a crank."

Prior to electricity and in the rural areas where home deliveries were not available for block ice, many in the western part of the state continued to use pans filled with a few inches of water to cool milk and eggs. Damp cheesecloth over a crock container did a surprisingly good job where the humidity stayed low enough to allow evaporation to work.

With electricity there soon came indoor plumbing, and the old mail order catalogues began to stack up. Propane (butane) gas modernized the rural area as natural gas had the cities. *The Lone Ranger* entertained the kids, and *Lum and Abner* and the *Screeching Door* occupied the grown-ups. The president held fireside chats in a two-million-square-mile living room. A guy named Joe Louis became the best boxer in the world.

Mr. Taylor had a business going in Philco radios at this time. "I'd sell one then I'd go out and install it," he said.

"What's to install about a radio," I asked.

"Well, often I'd have to go out on the roof and install an antenna for good reception. Anyway, about 1937 there was a heavyweight championship fight that everyone in the world was excited about. I think it was Joe Louis and Max Smelling, someone like that.

"There was a dealership down at Dallas that called me and said, 'Taylor, we've got hundreds of radios in here for repair and there isn't any way in the world we can get them all back to the customer by fight night. Everybody wants to hear that fight. Would you consider coming down here and helping us for the next six days? You just name your own wages.'"

"So you went to Dallas for a week."

"I did, and I learned a lot, too. That man they had in their shop was the best I ever saw. We set up an assembly line. I don't know how many radios we fixed, but it was a bunch."

Talking with Bedi made me look back to those times when the world changed rapidly. Refrigerators, radios, gas cookstoves, and hot water all came rushing in almost on top of each other. No more bathing in the kitchen in a number three wash tub—was it a number three? I'd not paid much attention. I had my own stuff going.

Soon to disappear were the smokehouses. For years they stood beside the main house with a single window through which meat could be handled. Inside were the cutting blocks and a big box, possibly three feet wide and nine feet long where meat was stored in ashes after smoking. Overhead, hooks and nails provided places for hanging meat while it smoked.

Mrs. C. Parks Casey from Brown County said, "Frequently porches extended from three sides of the house and a side porch had a flat tin roof where papers were spread to hold the peeled peaches to make dried fruit."

With the coming of electricity, the need for smokehouses rapidly disappeared. The new refrigerators provided better storage conditions for perishables, and the building beside the main structure, with a little alteration, became the garage for car or tractor.

With the teams out of the barn and the tractor in the smoke-house, the supply of used leather horse collars hanging on rafters around the countryside increased. Suddenly, no one minded the kids cutting the leather off them to make holsters for wooden guns. Now, the old harness hung on the rafters, taking the place of earlier reminders of World War I, things like army bandoleers, helmets, and gas masks that spoke of a horror too terrible to grasp.

For a while, in the more remote lanes, the highline boys left those long electric posts lying there beside gaping holes for days. Old Top would shy each time we loped past one. I'd claw for mane and pull myself upright and we'd keep going, but I should have known then what a job keeping life simple would become.

With electricity and well pumps and indoor plumbing, even Granny's place began to change. I had always thought of it as a crooked-nail place, but it had more class than about any mansion I ever saw. It had a windmill, a smokehouse, a two-hole privy, trees to climb, and a peach orchard. There just weren't many acres, and a hundred-acre farm was getting smaller by the minute in the late thirties.

If Granny's had been a cow outfit, I might have thought of it as a one-horse place. Dad's store was at a little jumping-off place. In the country names mean something.

For instance, the road widened at the store and a fellow could jump off a wagon there if he had to. And with good neighbors a one-horse spread can see after a few cattle. At Granny's we saved bent nails.

Now, not only was the harness useless and the tractor in the smokehouse, but my uncles filled in the trench under the toilet after plumbing the house. The clothesline still leaned and the wire drooped low, but Mother was the last jerked off the back of a horse ducking under that. With the team gone there was nothing to ride under there bigger than a dog, anyway. Down into the third generation by now, there was no way Great-granddad could have envisioned what a short time it took to dilute a paying operation when profit margins shrunk generation after generation.

Fortunately, the electric company relieved my generation from the monotony of creeping poverty. They came through the country digging those big highline postholes. My pals and I were only partially civilized in those days. The more siblings there were in the family, the less time the parents had to smooth the rough edges of the little ones. Also the more minds at work the more mischief could be created. Most families were large.

Two new kids moved in about the time these highline crews came through digging their holes. Differing from the norm, there were only two children in this family, one small boy of six years and his big brother of about fifteen. The older boy was huge. The newcomers answered to Smith.

The first day the Smith boys came to our three-room school, four brothers of another family put the smaller Smith boy in jail. For their cell they used the six-feet-deep posthole dug near school by the electric company. We all looked down in that hole and there that poor kid was, crying, mud and tear-streaked face turned up, sand falling down on him. The hole was large enough that he could stand comfortably and the danger was minimal, but he was one mad youngster.

Big brother came to the rescue like the U.S. Cavalry, and the fight started. He plowed into the biggest of the culprits with both fists swinging and the fight was underway. Big Smith against four brothers was an uneven match. The brothers needed one more sibling. The oldest of Smith's opponents matched him well in size, but the new guy had the strength of right and the fury of honest anger on his side. He bloodied three of the brothers until they wanted no more, and the fight ended with Smith and his oldest counterpart squared-off, one with an axe and the other with a sledgehammer from the coal bin. After a moment glaring at each other and wiping bloody noses on their shirtsleeve, they dropped the weapons. We all returned to class, long overdue from recess. The last to come in was big Smith, leading a sniffing little brother.

I don't remember anyone in that community ever bothering those boys again. Yet, war in all its fury awaited those older students. In the next battle, all involved were on the same side. And they crossed an ocean to get to the enemy.

WW II—
Total War

Monumental events sharpen the senses and crystallize memories. Simple scenes fix on mental film and frequently last a lifetime. A day meant to live in infamy qualifies as such a happening. Texans, nine years old on such a day, might recall stored images that included a balmy Sunday, playing on a cellar door, and ultimately the fatal radio message. Warm days, even in winter, are common in Texas; those as momentous as December 7, 1941, aren't.

Eugene Jones, a soldier in the Thirty-first Regiment's Anti-Tank Company heard of Pearl Harbor at 4 A.M., December 8 (Philippine time). Returning from an overnight pass to his post near Manila, he encountered a group of Filipino soldiers.

"They were running around like crazy, setting up roadblocks, and moving equipment. They told me the Japs had attacked Pearl Harbor and the United States was at war. When I got to my outfit the guys on sentry hadn't heard, but the word spread pretty fast.

"I believe it was the next day, maybe the next, some of them landed at Aparri and we started killing Japanese by the hundreds. We didn't have a lot to fight with, but we threw everything we had at them. The biggest was some .37mm anti-tank guns. The army issued all the Filipino men coconut-palm hats and a .45-caliber pistol. I mean revolvers, the Old-West-type six-shooters. Well, the Filipinos are a small race, and their hands are about half the size of ours." Jones drew an imaginary line across the palm of his hand. "They'd have to take both hands to shoot that thing, one to hold it and the other to pull the trigger." He shook his head.

Like Jones, William L. "Bill" Mann had already learned to soldier by Pearl Harbor Day. He'd been drafted into the army in July 1941. As part of the 80th Engineers of the 26th Engineering Battalion, he got the news en route to Camp Livingston, Louisiana. At that time Bill's specialty was water purification.

In Hattiesburg, Mississippi, his outfit had a short stop, and all they could hear was news of the Japanese attack. A buddy said, "Bill, you're the luckiest devil alive. They'll send women and kids to war before they send somebody to purify water." The next few years proved war hard to predict.

Another of America's fighting men, Paul Carter, like Jones and Mann, was already a member of the United States armed forces when the Japanese attacked Pearl Harbor. On January 3, 1940, he had volunteered for the Army Air Corps.

"By December 1941 everyone had heard the rumblings of war, but we gave it little thought. They'd used wooden guns to train us with, and no one serious about war would think that the word t-a-n-k written on the side of a duce-and-a-half truck was a serious operation.

"We were the 40th Fighter Squadron and as part of the 35th Fighter Group were stationed at Bear Field, Ft. Wayne, Indiana, that Sunday afternoon. The news broke about 2 P.M. Most guys were loitering around the barracks in civvies. We'd not been in Indiana long, but the 'clothes horses' had already pushed their credit to the limits buying out the local dry goods stores. Everyone wanted to know what and where Pearl Harbor was.

"We'd just been assigned Bell P-39 Airecobra fighters, but we had green pilots, and we were green mechanics. We didn't know from nothing! Most of us were out of there the next morning." Paul grinned, "I doubt those haberdashers ever saw much of what was owed on all those good-looking threads. We were headed west as fast as a green Air Corps could go."

Jones, already out there, added, "I'll say this, General MacArthur and Wainwright both knew what they were doing. For a year before, they'd had us surveying those islands. We established numbered concrete posts at every quarter-mile quadrant. Every spot on that island was zeroed in or pre-sighted for our guns."

Eugene sipped his coffee. "Anyway those first days of their offensive we were rationed two meals a day. There was no way for us to be resupplied. It wasn't long until we were down to one meal a day, and then in a few more days it was just whatever you could find to eat—dogs, monkeys, just anything. And add to that no sleep and dysentery.

"Some guys came down from the hills with their mules. Pretty soon the mules were all gone."

"You guys had left your horses in Texas with Patton," I said.

"Yeah, we had. You talk about good officers, that Patton was, just absolutely, the best. My folks received a letter from him when I was under his command saying he was proud to have me serving with him and if there was ever anything they needed to contact him."

Bill Mann added his own praise to Jones's admiration of Patton. Mann provided engineering support for the general's tanks near Bastogne. "Eisenhower was good and that Patton was a soldier's leader. He was the best. He didn't say go get 'em. He said follow me. That's what he said, 'follow me.' That's what an officer is supposed to do. He said, 'About this blood and guts thing, boys, it's your blood and my guts, c'mon.' He got a raw deal."

Returning the war to the Philippines, Jones described the situation before MacArthur's departure. "We had a little field hospital outfit with us down near the tip of the peninsula. It consisted of a few army nurses and maybe a half-dozen officers. Sometime around the first of April, they were to be evacuated.

Well some lieutenant was dating one of these nurses, and he slipped down there and dressed up in one of her uniforms to try to get out. They passed the word to shoot him on sight.

"April 9, 1942, we got word to destroy our equipment. I went to sleep or passed out, anyway a Japanese solder woke me up poking me. All I could see was that damn bayonet. He prodded around on me and made me get to my feet. They sent me to a hospital. At least, it was a place that had a bed and a window.

"A guy named Brown was in there with me, and after a few days we got to feeling a little better. The guards were around somewhere, but at this point they left us pretty much alone. This place had a window and I said, 'Brown, let's get out of here and beat our way up into them mountains.' In a minute we were out of there. We didn't make it though. We stumbled around for a while, but before long we ran into a gun emplacement full of Japs and they took us prisoner again.

"There was a Manchurian Japanese with this bunch that spoke English, but other than that, those guys didn't know anything. They had all this equipment, and it might as well have been from outer space for all they knew. They had half-tracks broken down all over that island. They had this interpreter ask me what I did in America.

"I said I was a mechanic. Well, I wasn't much of a mechanic, but I could tell I was a hell of a lot more of one than anything they had with them. They gave us an armband and a signed pass and told us to get in a jeep-like thing they had there and start driving. Anytime we came to a broken-down half-track we were to stop and try to fix it. They pointed at the band and said, 'You get stopped by Japanese patrol you show this then (motioning at the pass) show this.'

"So we had it pretty soft there for a few days. Then they moved us."

A sense of awe, like I was a little boy in the presence of an adult, became almost overpowering. "The Bataan death march?"

"Uh-huh, a lot of men died, a lot were killed. When somebody fell, if no one got there quick enough, they'd stick 'em. They were a mean people." Jones looked across the peaceful street. He lit a cigarette.

After twenty-nine days at sea aboard the USS *Ancon*, Paul Carter and the rest of the 40th Fighter Squadron arrived in Australia. "In June of 1942 we moved on to Port Moresby, New Guinea. I remember above the street leading to the docks was a big arch, and as our trucks passed under it, I read, 'Through these portals pass the best damn mosquito bait in the world.' They weren't kidding."

In spite of Jones's decision a few weeks earlier that the Japanese had little mechanical ability, Paul Carter soon became introduced to a phase of the war that told him the opposite. In terms of aircraft design, they were ahead. "A day's drive out of Port Moresby by truck and we arrived at our field. Our wait for an initiation to the war was a short one, only a few hours. Japanese Betty Bombers came over escorted by Zeroes. The bombers

Paul L. Carter in a P-47 on Gusap, New Guinea.

were at 20,000 feet and the fighters at 30,000. The highest our P-39s could go was about 15,000 feet. We had armor and self-sealing gas tanks. They had an advantage in altitude and maneuverability that left us sitting ducks for bombing raids for months.

"They bombed us at will. You see their planes had super-chargers and our aircraft didn't. We couldn't compete at high altitude. We just had to sit there and take those bombs. They weren't accurate, but they were sure as hell a nuisance. They wouldn't come every night, just intermittently. Our guys would go up, but they couldn't get that high.

"Finally we got two P-38s. Those babies were fine machines, and they had superchargers. We painted them black for night fighters and sent 'em up each night to just wait. After a couple of nights, here came the Japs. Our two guys came sweeping down from above and pretty soon we could see tracers going all over that sky. We just lay there in our foxholes and watched the show. You talk about surprised Japs! Our guys let 'em have it. After that, things began to improve, at last we felt like we could hold our own with them."

Paul explained the Owen-Stanley mountain range was all that separated them from the Japanese army. "No one thought it humanly possibly for them to cross those mountains. They did. The word was they resorted to cannibalism to get to us, but one day they were there. Were it not for the U.S. the Japanese would have taken Australia. That time, the Aussies saved us. After that the battle of the Coral Sea gave us relief and the tempo of the war changed."

About 400 miles west and north of Paul Carter's position on New Guinea, W. D. Hines fought Japanese. He was a member of a United States segregated army artillery outfit. His war took place on an island named Biak, a part of the Netherland East Indies.

I mentioned the Japanese scaling the Owen-Stanley moun-tain range over near Paul Carter's field. "We had a mountain there on Biak, also, but they didn't cross it. They tunneled through it."

He explained, "The island is about seven by fourteen miles. They dug a tunnel, about seven miles, through this mountain and put a track in there and mounted heavy artillery on the track. That thing was big. And our planes, our guns, nothing could get at it in that tunnel. When the navy would bring a ship close, that gun would open up. We had 90mm pieces and we could do a number on their air attacks, but that tunnel was a problem.

"I guess by today's standards, we were old-fashioned. You see we'd cut our shells down to control the height we wanted to fire. You wanted them to go a little lower you cut a little more off. But you wanted to stay out of the way of that breech block's recoil. That thing came back and would really get you.

"Oh, they dropped a lot of bombs, but at the height they came over, they didn't do much damage. Well, most of them anyway, all but the 'daisy-cutter.'"

"What was that?"

"It was a fragmentation bomb. It tore things up pretty bad."

"What did you do, just finally have to go in and dig those guys out of that tunnel?" I asked.

"Uh-huh! We couldn't take machine guns in with us because of the way they ricocheted in there, especially the tracers. We finally dug them out with just M-1s, hand grenades, and flame throwers."

T-3 grade Jack Spann with the 30th Evacuation Hospital in New Guinea knew the Japanese to be a terrible foe. Attached to the 7th Australian Division, he found another about as deadly and even more difficult to see was a mite that caused the often-fatal typhus fever. "One bite of this tiny insect and after a twenty-one-day incubation period, the strongest soldier became seized with a fever. In many cases, with better food and conditions it wouldn't have been so bad. With what we had at hand it often proved fatal."

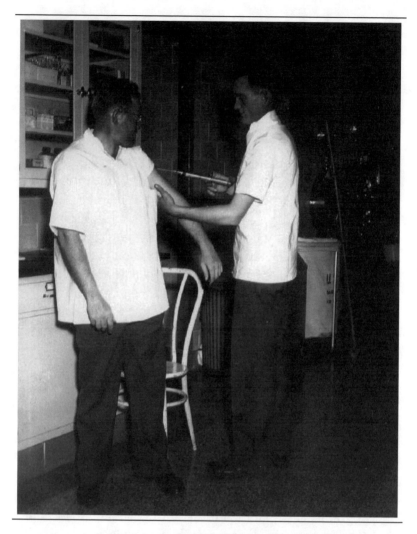

Jack Spann on the good end of the syringe (right).

Jack's outfit also served with the 5th Regiment of the 1st Marines on the island of New Britain. After becoming ill, Jack found himself recuperated but without transportation a couple of hundred miles away from his outfit. "I was there thirty-two or thirty-three days waiting on transportation for just 200 miles. Finally I got a ride on a ship manned by locals."

"They let me off on this dock and I found some MPs who told me our medical unit was a couple of hundred yards up the road. I took off hiking up there, and the first guy I met was the 1st sergeant.

"'Where the hell you been?' He asked."

Jack thumbed through his photo album looking for the right picture. "I got a friend in here I want to show you. He married one of our nurses. He says I saved his life. I tell him, no, I just cleaned you up some. She saved your life. We talk on the phone every week."

Eugene Jones continued detailing his experience as a POW. "I arrived in Japan on Thanksgiving day, 1942. Cold, my God! They put us to work on a dam. A lot more men died. There wasn't much to eat. After the dam, I was sent to a carbide smelter. By this time I had learned Japanese pretty good. They used me some for an interpreter. There was one guard there we called Big 'Glass-eye.' He was mean."

"You mentioned once being threatened with execution. How'd that come about?" I asked.

"It was more than once, but the time you speak of, I insulted Tojo," Jones said.

"You what?"

"Insulted Tojo."

"What did you do, say something bad about his white horse?" I asked.

"No, that was the emperor. You remember that old ditty? Claxton did this Claxton did that." Jones's expression said he struggled with uncertain memories. "'The Wreck of the Ninety-Seven,' I believe that was it. Well I substituted Tojo's name for Claxton and was singing that one day when a guard overheard me. They hauled me in and beat me, maybe a couple of hours, but I kept getting up. Then they had this wooden bookshelf thing, and they started hitting me with that thing. Pretty soon

my head was big as a basketball. They were some stirred up."
Jones shook his head in memory of his own lack of prudence.

"Then this Jap officer said, 'In the morning, we shoot you.'
He nodded and they drug me off to my cell."

Jones laughed. "You know, in thirty minutes they were
bringing me soft food, stuff that I could eat, and I never heard
another word. We had a captain with us and I think he talked to
them, but I don't know."

"How'd you get word the war was over?" I asked.

"It was there at the carbide plant. They had me welding on
the fan inside this big concrete mixer. It was cool so at noon I
curled up inside the thing and caught some snoozes. This guard
I knew woke me up beating the butt of his rifle against the outside of the mixer saying in Japanese, 'I surrender, me surrender.
War is over.'"

"I said, 'Give me your damn rifle.' Damned if he didn't hand
it over."

"You got a little different treatment after that." I said.

"I did," he nodded. "I was six feet tall and weighed ninety-
seven pounds when they got me to the hospital."

Jones made a career of the military after that, serving in
both the air force and the army. Later he spent another twenty
with the Dallas police department. Intrigued by the brass and
sheer gall of his act of defiance, I checked out the ditty he sang
to his captors. It turned out his memory did throw him a curve
and it was the last stanza of "The Wabash Cannonball" he sere-
naded his guards with.

Actual Version
Here's to Daddy Claxton, may his name forever stand
And always be remembered in the courts throughout the
land.
His earthly days are over and the curtains around him fall
They'll carry him home to victory on the Wabash
Cannonball.

POW Version
Here's to Daddy Tojo, may his name forever stand
And always be remembered in the cesspools of the land.
His earthly days are over and the curtains around him fall
They'll carry him home to hell on the Wabash Cannonball.

The first five years of the decade of the forties were, for our country and our state, unlike the past and different from the future. That era formed the narrows, the watershed, between the old and the new. Win the war and all things were possible. Lose the war and all was lost. It and the years before were not a time of innocence or simplicity; fear, uncertainty, perhaps never equaled, hovered like a cloud above the people. Control of democracy's destiny sank with the big ships at Pearl Harbor. The country, like our allies, united to win a war.

Still, the opportunity for human avarice flourished with profiteering, draft dodging, and unfaithfulness. Marriages suffered, and the breakup of relations became so common that the meaning of "Dear John" became known to all. Parents, children, and spouses joined their beloved soldiers as emotional casualties of war.

Disaster breeds scam artists, nourishes the baser instincts, and this one was no exception. Women married servicemen for their allotments and were never seen again. The looters, the slackers, the shamed always prowl the fringes, but considering the enormity of the situation, their numbers were small. Some cut corners, sometimes hoarding rationed items, but they went to work, and they bought bonds. Americans wrote to loved ones in uniform, cried, and prayed for them. Empty chairs at family gatherings and starred flags hanging in windows were constant reminders of the absent servicemen they represented. Their absence left holy voids in the souls of all their loved ones. No human frailty could compete for the energy needed to protect the man at the front. His needs, if they could possibly be satisfied, took precedence over all.

The Mafia joined hands with the FBI against espionage. Bootleggers bought war bonds, and criminals left their cells to enter the war. Women went to work, and scientists experimented late into the night. Humanity's future hung in the balance. Inconceivable evil gnawed at the basic tenets of civilization.

While the people at home did their best and Eugene Jones faced the uncertainty of death at the whim of his tormentors in Japan, Bill Mann watched as the islands of England and Scotland became more and more packed in preparation for the invasion of Normandy. As part of the 26th Engineering Battalion, he shipped out with the outfit from Fort Dix, New Jersey, and landed in Belfast, Ireland. Billeted in castles at various times in Ireland and then later in Scotland, Bill discovered real darkness with constant blackouts and few clear nights.

Bottom row left to right: William (Bill) Mann, James Simmons, Russell Barnes, Don Williams, Lester Anderson, Reed Allen, Dave Waszel, George Kruzich. Top row left to right: Howard Tharp, Elmer Supe, Elmer Jones, Ray Mornson, Max Sorenson, Charles Moore.

50th Anniversary Council

The Battle of Normandy Foundation
is proud to appoint:

Mr. Wiliam L. Mann

Member of the 50th Anniversary Council for
the Battle of Normandy.

As such, this Council Member shall help plan and celebrate the
50th Anniversary of the Battle of Normandy which began
June 6, 1944. This celebration will honor all American veterans who
fought and sacrificed to preserve world freedom.

Senator Strom Thurmond
Director

Anthony C. Stout
President

Letter from Senator Thurmond.

Month after month they trained for the invasion of France. They knew they were going. The Germans knew they were coming, but neither knew where. Still, in an engineering outfit, it became apparent that when they got to their destination only the Germans would be in front of them. They were training with explosives for the purpose of blowing up underwater mines and obstacles at the water's edge, clearing a landing zone for amphibious vehicles. When their initial work was complete, the engineers still standing would go up on the beach with the infantry and rangers.

Bill spoke rapidly, "For weeks the Air Force had been bombing up the coast to make the Germans think we were going in there. They'd make about three attacks up at Calais for each one down at Normandy. Finally we loaded up, planning to land on June 5, 1944. We carried a full pack, all our equipment, and twenty-five pounds of TNT fastened to every man. It was like we had an anchor in our pocket.

"The weather turned awful. Omaha Beach was our zone. We had to clear it, had to make a place for those LCT, LST, the LCVPs. We had to blow those barriers out of there. The weather worsened and we pulled back at the last moment.

"The BBC blew the whole thing. They announced on June the fifth, 'At this moment, as we speak, our allies are storming the beaches at Normandy.' Well, that was the plan at one time. We went in on June 6, but it seemed every German in Europe had listened to the BBC and got there the night before.

"We went in on a LCVP and you could hear the sailor marking the depth. Five feet, six feet, three feet—you see, the bow of that thing was bouncing up and down. Anyway we must have gone in on a ledge with a drop-off. So many of the guys just dropped plumb out of sight. No way they could swim, just too much weight, right straight down they went. It was awful. And the Germans up on that hill shooting right down on us." Bill took a breath, looked across his beloved cemetery.

"The Rangers got up those cliffs some way, and this destroyer, God bless her heart! I don't know who they were, but that skipper sailed the thing right up near the beach and just sailed right up and down, just off that beach, shooting point blank into those pillboxes and gun emplacements. God bless their hearts, you talk about brave!

"Well after that we fought our way inland. You've heard of the hedgerows. Well, we were in 'em. They were terrible. I remember coming to some woods once and they had a sniper in a tree that gave him a view of the road we were on. He had a perfect spot, dark in behind him and our guys out on that road.

"Well, we had a sergeant with us that had a nose like a birddog. That man could smell an egg. When we'd leave a farmhouse this guy would have eggs in every pocket, in his britches, everywhere. Well, the sergeant was on a truck when this sniper started in on us. When he got close enough, the sergeant jumped off and over a ditch and rolled onto his belly. He got the sniper then yelled, 'Oh, my God! My eggs.' He started feeling of his clothing. As God is my witness, he'd not broken a one. Well, we'd been scared so long we just lost control laughing at this guy." Bill rubbed his eyes.

"I think we took Saint Lo about five times then later, near Paris, we stopped and waited to let the Free French take the city. I remember sitting there and watching all these Frenchmen come rolling by on tanks we'd given them. There wasn't an empty spot on any of them. French men and women waving wine bottles and singing, hugging, and kissing. I don't know... but they took the city." Bill coughed and cleared his throat, obviously anxious to continue. He refused an offer of water.

"At one time these English-speaking Germans infiltrated our lines dressed in American uniforms. They caused a lot of damage, and it got to where you couldn't be sure if you were asking a German or an American for a light for your cigarette. We started asking each other things like, 'What would you do for a Camel?'—Walk a mile of course. Another was, 'Who's in

Brooklyn?'—The Bums of course. If you were slow with your answer you might end up shot.

"The Germans launched a counteroffensive and overran a new outfit that hadn't been on the front long. Sort of green and arrogant, these guys had been putting this stuff on us about we could relax now they were here and everything like that. Those Germans came through, and you never saw a bunch of guys run so fast in your life. Man they were fast. I know, because I was trying to catch them." Mann burst into laughter.

Involved in one of those German counteroffensives was Vivian Hess' husband, Gilbert. "I understand he was an acting sergeant that day. He was hit in the back with shrapnel, near the spine. It left him with a stiff leg for a long time. Slowly, a bit at a time, its use came back. As soon as he could travel, he came home.

"He'd prepared me with letters, but I wasn't sure I'd know him. I knew he would be on crutches. I saw him get out of the car. My fears of lack of recognition were well founded. I probably wouldn't have known him. He'd lost seventy-five pounds, but he was home."

Bill said, "Well, when it was over I had 121 points. They rotated us out based on a point system. With all those points I just knew I'd be home in no time. What do you think, we were after the dogs, cats, chickens; everybody got home before we did. They put us on the USS *Pegasus*, a transport. I think that was its name, we called it the 'Beetle Goose.'"

Bill directed me toward the flagpole where he raises the flag each morning and then lowers it in the evening. On the way he pointed out a simple stone that marked the site of his beloved wife's grave. A few yards down the winding road the flagpole stood above several dozen veterans' graves. We were in Waco, Texas. There were signs of recent fills of dirt and other corrections to tombstone positions that Bill acknowledged as being his work.

"I do this now for my buddies," he said. "They deserve it. It is the job I've assigned myself.

"Now, I want to give some flowers to the living," he said. "We did what needed to be done, but every man, woman, and child in America was helping us. We didn't lack for anything that was in their power to get for us. There was none of this party bickering, none of this them versus us."

It is not easy to say "so-long" to a Bill Mann. Somehow, a person wants to stay near him. You feel safe in his shadow. Still, it's comforting to know where one man will be at sunup tomorrow.

William "Bill" Mann.

The Way We Lived It

World War II ended with blasts from a new era. Two atomic bombs, totaling less than ten tons in weight, saved a prolonged harvest of human life by eliminating the need to invade Japan. In the eyes of many, the last war won by our nation, it ended in victory due to the character, courage, and dedication represented by the old-time Texans, their siblings from other states, and their allied counterparts around the world. These people's willingness to fight, produce, sacrifice, and create became in the end unstoppable.

It was time for a new beginning. It was time for the living to come home and the dead to rest. The world cause had been achieved, and a new dynamic power pulsed around the globe. The fight had been fought because there was no alternative and with no assurance as to its outcome. Victory or death is a simple equation. Perhaps, that is the lesson—total commitment or no war.

During the last years of the conflict, not only did our scientists build a powerful bomb, but they also developed a scientific methodology that offered much for the next faltering steps of man through the last half of the twentieth century. Soon at Bell Laboratories, scientists performed interesting work in the study of semiconductors. During the war years in Texas, a young industrial dogie recently branded Geophysical Services Inc. scampered through one discovery after another. Soon to be renamed Texas Instruments Incorporated and with a Bell Labs license, this young upstart would hit the markets with products once thought impossible and spawn satellite companies to provide the world with unimaginable wonders. With a generation prepared by the remarkable model of the last of the old-time Texans, the state marched into a new era and away from it agricultural and mineral roots. High-tech stampeded across the land.

Thirty-one years later in Humble, Texas, near Moonshine Hill, a lady of grace and warmth sounded taps for the old ways and pointed to the new. Asked to tell of her life by the writers of *A History of the Humble Texas Area*. Mrs. Pruitt did so.

Mary Lois Banks married Henry Pruitt. In her words, "We were blessed with five children, Mary Alee, William 'Bill,' Emma Ophelia, Henry Albert Jr., and Ora Elizabeth." Mary and Henry Pruitt Sr. made their home in Humble.

In relating her history Mrs. Pruitt discussed each of her children, her grandchildren, and then her great-grandchildren. She recorded highlights and times, good and bad, on Moonshine Hill. The personalities of her family and those who married into it were presented in a loving and generous manner.

Mrs. Pruitt said, "Mary was born on August 9, 1908. One night when she was about eight months old and she wasn't feeling too well, I had put her on the bed and was trying to soothe her and get her off to sleep. Henry was in the front room reading the Bible, and I kept hearing a noise that sounded like a baby crying or possibly a kitten. I stood it as long as I could and then picked Mary up in my arms and went to the door, and there on our porch was a small baby.

"What happened next still frightens me. I ran outside, sat Mary down, picked up the other child, and ran in to show Henry. When I realized what I had done, I ran back and picked Mary up. It was a long time before I could forget having left her on the porch alone for any time at all.

"The orphaned baby was left with only a blanket, flour sack diaper, and a can of milk. But by evening the next day, neighbors had brought clothes and everything a child could possibly need.

The baby was a little boy, and we judged he was about the same age as Mary.

"We felt we could not adequately care for another child, and so many wanted to adopt this adorable baby. Well, the laws were not like they are today, so it became our lot to decide to whom the orphan should be given.

"There was a couple in the neighborhood who, it was believed, could not have children and it was this couple we chose. Ironically, the woman got pregnant shortly after getting this little boy.

"The baby, the little orphan, did not live long, and no one really knows why it died. The adopted mother was hanging clothes on the line when a woman came and asked if she could see the baby, which was not unusual because everyone was interested in the child. Anyway the baby died within a short time after this woman left the house. I wonder..."

She concluded, "Fatal tragedy struck our lives for the first time when we lost Mary, but we were again to feel its sting when Henry, husband and daddy of this family, graduated from this world by death at the age of seventy-four, on March 3, 1963. His going, as always, was to join our daughter, Mary, and thereby pave the way for us and to wait with our loved ones until we, too, will make our way from this earth to be with him, our loved ones, and Jesus Christ.

"You will notice I have put him first in those waiting for us, but during the time he spent on earth, he would not permit any of his children to call him 'Father.' His belief was that we only have one Father and he was merely their daddy.

"As our feeble efforts to put my life and loves on paper are being made, we have at one other time felt the sting of tragedy. This was when our beloved Larry, son of Pete and Ophelia, leaving us with two beautiful great-grandchildren, also graduated from this life in 1964. What a joy Larry had been to all of us. His two small sons were Randy and Stephen 'Corky' and his wife was Lena May, the wife he adored and, we felt at the time, he married too young. But in retrospect, how glad we are that Ophelia and Pete had the foresight to give their blessings to this marriage, one truly made in Heaven. Now Randy has married and, of all things, has given us a great-great-granddaughter.

'Some only think of toils and sorrows,
I prefer to remember the happy hours.'
This is the way we lived it and loved it."

I called Dad yesterday. The Cowboys had just beaten the Eagles. He said he was doing fine, picking pecans and watching the highlights. It's twelve days before Christmas—the last one this century. That must mean its time to wrap this. As I finished Mrs. Pruitt's words those of others from our tally sheet came reverberating back at me. What a wondrous trail they forged.

****

"And this chasm which has been naught to me,
To that fair-haired youth may a pitfall be.
Good friend I'm building this bridge for him."

****

"Run him as long as he'll run, but bring back the doctor."

****

"I ain't putting this man's cattle in no dry lot."

****

"We'll carry him home to hell on the Wabash Cannonball."

****

"All five grew to be fine young men, and I'm proud to say, none ever served a day in the pen or the legislature."

****

"What's a man's last duty to his fellow man?"

****

"My only regret is I lived a hundred years too soon."

****

"She needn't have bothered, for he hid a bottle in our barn and came and checked our cow each afternoon."

****

"I was blessed, and the good Lord, he don't ever give you no more grief than good times."

The End

Old-Timer's Tally Sheet

Biographies, Interviews, and Excerpts

BAIR, NOVA SCHUBERT. Interviewed November 9, 1999, Garland.

Nova was born at Dodge City, Kansas, on January 5, 1911. Moving west, her Missouri-raised parents settled first in the Oklahoma Panhandle then relocated in Hansford County in the Texas Panhandle. Earlier, Nova's dad had been on a train, en route to California to purchase land, when someone talked him into appraising the North Plains of the Panhandle areas of Texas and Oklahoma.

"When he discovered he could set a plow and turn a furrow as far as you could see, it was enough to convince him to stay," Nova said.

Receiving big doses of inspiration and aptitude from both her fiddle-playing father and Bible-loving mother, Nova learned to whistle tunes before she talked and was writing poems at the age of nine.

She moved with her family to Burkburnett during the oil boom in a covered wagon. A few years later an automobile provided the power for the return trip to the North Plains. She was working for the Magnolia Oil Company in Amarillo and participating in the Civic Chorus when she met fellow musician Clyde Bair. The music was Handel's *Messiah*, and the acquaintance turned to love. The two were married and made their home in Amarillo.

Nova attended West Texas State University and the Musical Arts Conservatory of Amarillo and holds a Bachelor of Music degree. She taught piano and theory at the Musical Arts Conservatory for many years and is also a published writer of poetry.

While others of her generation nourished the state's plants and animals, built the highways and structures, or healed the sick, Nova brought Beethoven to life in the Panhandle. She proved culture as enriching and comfortable in Texas jeans as it is in Eastern top hats.

CARTER, PAUL L. Interviewed October 27, 1999, Garland.

Paul was born in Leaksville, North Carolina, on September 28, 1921. In the U.S. Air Corps when World War II started, he first saw Texas as a young air force man in December 1941. His outfit limped into Love Field only a few days after Pearl Harbor en route to the West Coast and ultimately New Guinea.

"We were in Dallas three days due to rain and many maintenance problems, the new disc brakes were the major headache. Our permanent base had been Bear Field, Fort Wayne, Indiana. From Dallas we flew to Los Angles then up to Payne Field near Everett, Washington. To show how unprepared the country was for war, even the Air Corps, the ordeal of moving just those few P-39s across country took us nineteen days and several wrecked fighters plus others grounded waiting on parts. Nineteen of us mechanics flew in a C-47. Still, for the military that was sort of dizzying speed for we were on the West Coast before New Years 1942."

Carter's outfit ultimately arrived in New Guinea, and there they found plenty of war. If they were green troops when the war started, by the time Paul accumulated enough points for rotation out of the South Pacific battle zone, he was a seasoned veteran who knew his role and the planes he kept in the air. To utilize that experience the Air Corps reassigned him to the P-47 training base at Major's Field in Greenville, Texas.

Paul described the day he got the word he would rotate out as one of "hope." He now had a chance to outlast the war. In Greenville he met and married a Texas girl.

CONINE, DOYLE. Interviewed November 19, 1999, Garland.

Born 15 December 1913 in Fannin County, Doyle's family moved across the Red River to Blue, Oklahoma. He said, "The insects ran us out of that country when I was seven years old, and we came back to Texas in a truck that was chain driven and had solid tires. My uncle had a dray-line business in Sherman and used trucks of that type as well as teams."

Back in Texas the family settled on a farm near Josephine, and Conine grew to manhood in the depth of the Depression. Work was hard to find, and he remembers hitchhiking and hopping freights while searching for jobs.

Doyle retired from the construction industry and now lives in Garland. He enjoys a good laugh, and we visited one afternoon and shared a number of his humorous stories. "Early on, an old man up in Oklahoma got some money together and bought him one of those Model-A trucks. Wal, he didn't get home before he ran that thing square into the creek.

"A man came by and helped pull him out. It was a straight road and dry so the good neighbor asked, 'What happened?'

"The old man poured water out of his hat and shook his head. 'Wal I looked up the road and here come that bridge, lickety-split, straight at me. I missed her, but that dern creek got me.'"

CRAWFORD, DR. W. V., deceased. Excerpts from Juanita Daniel Zachry and others, *Taylor County*, Nortex Press, Burnett, 1980.

Dr. Crawford completed his medical training at Louisville Medical College then came to Buffalo Gap in 1887. He practiced there for many years. Impatient with the old ways, he chaffed at the lack of remedies available to him and the delays involved in getting to his patients.

Interviewed in 1923, he was proud of Abilene's hospital and the development of automobiles that enabled him to reduce his response time to the bedside of those who needed him. Still apparently a man of vision, he seemed to recognize the great strides in medicine waiting just around the corner.

CUMMINGS, MRS. CHARLES GORDON, MARY THOMAS, deceased. Excerpts from Mrs. Clyde Warwick and others, *The Randall County Story*, Pioneer Publishers, Hereford, 1969.

Mrs. Cummings was born March 3, 1878, in Dallas County. She arrived in Amarillo as a young art teacher in September 1899. The following year she visited in the home of Mr. and Mrs. Charles Goodnight at their ranch in Palo Duro Canyon.

"I remember so well the evening meal!" She said, "The way the lemonade looked in the pitcher—there was milk in a pitcher, too, homemade light bread, fresh roast beef, honey from their own hives, turnip greens growing in the garden, and jelly and fruits from the orchard."

Mary later married Charles Lennox Gordon Cummings and ultimately became known as the last of the widows of old-time T Anchor Ranch cowboys. She and Charles made their home at Canyon, Texas, and she received a multitude of awards and well-deserved recognition for her many contributions to that area. Mary died in 1972.

CUMMINS, DR. DAVE L., deceased. Excerpts from Rex A. Felker and others, *Haskell County and Its Pioneers*, Nortex Press, Quanah, 1975.

Dr. Cummins was born October 28, 1866, in Jackson County, Tennessee. The son of a farmer and a miller of grain and in spite of a rough ending to his first year's schoolwork, he advanced far beyond the amount of schooling most of his generation obtained.

His daughter LaVern wrote, "Little Dave was noticed stumbling and falling as he approached home. It turned out the young teacher had celebrated the end of the school year by passing his jug around among his pupils."

After receiving his M.D. from the University of Nashville and Vanderbilt, Dr. Cummins packed his medical instruments and headed for Texas. Soon afterward he married Lena Maude Davis and they made their home in Bell County.

In 1907 they moved to Haskell, and he practiced there for many years. Dr. Cummins died January 2, 1943.

CURTIS, NORRIS. Interviewed October 11, 1999, Nevada.

Mr. Curtis was born in Nevada, Texas, in 1915. His grandfather managed to acquire 1,700 acres of good, black farmland in that area. Norris loved the farm life and left school as soon as he put together enough coin to purchase a team of mules.

I found him in 1999 living on the same site he was born on. He shared a number of his thoughts and memories. I am in debt to this old-time historian for many interesting stories of the locale he groomed for a lifetime.

HAMER, FRANK, CAPTAIN TEXAS RANGERS. Excerpts from E. R. Milner's, *The Lives and Times of Bonnie and Clyde*, Southern Illinois University Press, 1996.

Born in 1884, Frank received national attention as the leader of the posse that brought Bonnie Parker and Clyde Barrow to the end of their bloody crime spree in May 1934. Weighing over 200 pounds, the six-foot-plus, heavy-smoking ex-Ranger captain exemplified Texas law enforcement of that day. Governor Miriam Ferguson assigned him Special Agent specifically to apprehend the two fugitives.

Having studied his quarry, Frank set his trap. The night before the final gun battle he reported the following simple message to his boss, director of the Texas Prison System, Lee Simmons. "The old hen is about ready to hatch. I think the chickens will come off tomorrow."

Later that day souvenir hunters and an exuberant crowd were almost berserk in the small Louisiana town where the autopsy was being performed. The reticent lawman's public comments were limited to, "Well, they died with their guns in their hands."

Upon the arrival of his boss, he added, "Okay, boys, here is the boss. I've been acting on his instructions and any general statement will come from him." This was at a time when half of the lawmen on the scene were hogging cameras and claiming responsibility for the successful conclusion of the dangerous mission.

Frank remained in law enforcement and security work. He held an interest in a security company in Houston until his retirement in 1949. He retired to Austin and after suffering a heatstroke from which he never recovered, he died at age seventy-one in 1955.

HESS, MRS. GILBERT R., VIVIAN HELMS. Interviewed November 17, 1999, Garland.

Born February 2, 1923, in Josephine, Vivian fulfilled her childhood dream and became a schoolteacher. She remembered sharing her teaching aspirations with two friends. One of the other girls' greatest goals was to go abroad and see, in particular, countries bordering the Mediterranean. Later, as personal secretary and companion to the wife of her cousin, Audie Murphy, this friend achieved her goal.

The third member of the three sharers of secrets wanted the impossible. Her dream was to be married to a wealthy man and be mistress of an enormous home. She was later married to a man who owned shopping centers and valuable real estate.

Vivian's husband served in Europe in the Second World War and was wounded in the Battle of the Bulge. He wrote of his wound and told her, "You are going to have a shock when you see me." Not knowing what to expect, she was in fact surprised to see his new mustache.

HINES, W. D. Interviewed November 11, 1999, Garland.

A (Disciples of Christ) Christian Church pastor, Rev. Hines was born of farm "sharecropper" parents at Bryan in 1922. When I met W. D. in 1999 he was employed full time at the job he had held for forty-five years with former Chuck Howley's and now Lee Roy Jordan's Uniform Company. Sundays find him preaching at his Greenville church.

W. D. served the United States during World War II as a soldier in the segregated army of that time. He was engaged in heavy South Pacific combat in the Netherland East Indies. W. D. said, "I was lucky. I escaped being hurt." Recalling the funerals, the hundreds of weddings, the week after week of sermons, and the example of his life, one must wonder if there wasn't more blessing than luck involved in his destiny.

In 1992 Mr. and Mrs. Hines celebrated fifty years of marriage, an event that celebrated what one reporter termed a "Cotton-Patch wedding." "She was picking cotton when we met, not pulling, picking."

"What about you, were you picking?" I asked.

"Me, I didn't like picking cotton. Man I was wearing starched and ironed khakis when I saw her. I went out there and asked her would she go with me. At first she didn't want to. She said 'No.' Well, you bet I started picking that lint and adding it to her sack. Directly she said, 'Wal, alright.'"

JACKSON, MRS. LESSIE HODGES (my grandmother). Interviewed prior to 1975, Knox County.

Born in 1887, Granny later moved as a child to Knox County with her family. She married Jim Jackson, a farmer, on or about 1903, and they brought eight children into the world. One child died prior to age two.

A heart attack took Granddad in 1937, at age fifty-six, and Grandmother, with the aid of the three younger boys, continued farming. Surviving in a world where bent nails were treasured and the hammer handle broken, she insisted her family drive their nails of life straight and deep. Filled with a pioneering spirit, an indomitable will, and a love of the land, she was called Granny by most in her neighborhood.

In her world, life's circle contained a strong religious faith, family values, work, and the land. She struggled for many years to keep her circle intact. During the Second World War, the flag in her window held two service stars, and at its end she was blessed with the return of both sons. Those of us left behind flounder in the void of her absence and struggle with the circle she drew, bending here, twisting there, sometime challenging, not always convinced, but definitely influenced by her values. She died in 1975.

JONES, EUGENE. Interviewed October 8, 1999, Garland.

Eugene Jones was born March 2, 1920, near Farmersville in Collin County. A tough, independent, small-town youngster conditioned by hard Depression years, Eugene joined the army on November 18, 1938. Assigned to the 5th U.S. Horse Cavalry, the young inductee soon found himself stationed at Fort Clark, Texas.

Jones said, "At this time, Lt. General Jonathan M. Wainwright was the post commander, and his adjutant was George Patton."

The fifth had a couple of half-track field vehicles. Other than that, it was all horse mounted. Jones soon found himself assigned to Wainwright as his field driver. In the latter part of '39 the 5th was transferred to Fort Bliss at El Paso. Horses and men arrived there after passing through Balmorhea and Fort Davis.

In early 1940 Jones volunteered for overseas duty then found himself in the old walled city of Manila in the Philippine Islands. Soon, to his surprise, he reunited with General Wainwright. Having been given a not too complementary description of duty in the Philippines by the general before leaving El Paso, Jones asked. "What are you doing here?"

"I don't run this damn army yet, Son," the general said.

In 1941, as a part of the Thirty-first Infantry Regiment's Anti-Tank Co., Jones found himself eating monkey when lucky, sleeping once a week, and constantly killing Japanese. Sick, starved, and unconscious when the allied forces were overrun, Jones awoke to being kicked and poked. A Japanese bayonet beckoned him to his feet. For him, Wainwright, and the remnants of the U.S. forces in that area, their gallant battle had ended.

Eugene's strength and will were tested beyond modern comprehension by the Bataan death march and the subsequent years as a POW in both the Philippines and Japan. Six feet tall and weighing ninety-seven pounds when freed, Mr. Jones is one of the last remaining members of his old company. The word survivor was coined for him. He is one of the creditors for all our freedom.

A young shot-up marine, fresh back from Korea, once told me, "The word 'hero' only belongs on grave markers." If Pruitt is wrong, that word, too, should be part of Mr. Jones' title. But only if Pruitt is wrong, for Jones will tell you, he's much alive today.

MANN, WILLIAM L. "BILL." Interviewed October 14, 1999, Waco.

Bill was born April 18, 1919, in Oglesby, near Waco. He was given his Methodist-preaching great-grandfather's name. Mann showed an early interest in the military by becoming a member of the National Guard while in high school. "It took a lot of doing, but I finally talked Mother into letting me join the navy at age seventeen. It was December 19, 1937, and I lacked one year finishing school."

Bill did a tour in the navy, serving aboard the destroyers the USS *Brooks* and the USS *Davis*. He had been home with a discharge only a few months when he was drafted into the army in July 1941.

Bill stormed ashore as one of the first Americans on Omaha Beach on D-Day, June 6, 1944. Fighting gallantly throughout the balance of the war in Europe, Bill returned home, married, and lived a productive life in Waco.

Bill's devotion to his fallen comrades caught the attention of many Texans when a Metroplex TV station carried a short human-interest story on him in 1999. For no pay and out of a sense of duty to his old buddies, Bill raises and lowers the flag over the graves of veterans in Waco. He honored me with an interview and even more with his friendship.

MURDOCK, J. T. "JAKE" (my father). Interviewed 1999, Seymour.

Born January 15, 1910, in Wood County, Murdock moved to Knox County as a teenager. The working son of a farmer, J. T. grew to strength and stature beyond most of his generation. At over six feet and weighing near two hundred pounds, finding work on threshers and then highway jobs at age fourteen presented no problem. Surviving days unloading boxcars filled with steel at bridge sites gave him cause to pause and consider other livelihoods.

Like so many of his peers, his schooling stopped after the fifth grade so he could work full time. At eighteen he married Opal Mae Jackson. They sealed their wedding vows with a commitment that their children would have better educational advantages than they knew. During the next few years, Dad worked on the infant road systems in both East and West Texas, at cotton gins, and on farms.

After discovering the vehicle owner earned more than the one handling the shovel, he bought his first truck before age twenty-five. As an independent contractor, hauling gravel, furniture, grain, cotton, and cattle, he became one of the first truckers roaming the pavement and gravel roads west of Fort Worth. Livestock traders taught him their trade and kept him busy with four-hundred-mile round trips to the Fort Worth stockyards.

At twenty-eight, Dad bought a country grocery store. At thirty-eight he sold that and bought a farm. He and mother lived to realize their dream of putting their children through college and surprised themselves by having enough left to retire at age sixty-five.

MURDOCK, LORA (WISDOM). Interviewed October 20, 1999, Seymour.

Born February 14, 1909, in Knox County, Lora and her sister Flora opened the first beauty parlors in both Goree and Bomarton, Texas. Those shops were opened in 1928. Later, except for the years of World War II she operated a beauty shop in Seymour. Lora's first husband, Earl Wisdom, preceded her in death and she later married J. T. Murdock whose own wife had passed away earlier. Lora taught children's Sunday school continuously at Seymour's First Baptist Church for fifty years. At the time of this writing in 1999, she is in good health and active.

MURDOCK, MRS. NETTIE BROWN (grandmother). Interviewed prior to 1975, Dallas.

Grandmother was born in Wood County and later married Sid Murdock. Dad had two older brothers and two younger brothers and a sister. One of the younger brothers died in infancy. Grandmother was gentle in her manners, strong in her faith, and possessed a good sense of humor.

As young wife and mother, she traveled through downtown Dallas en route to West Texas in a covered wagon drawn by a team. Granddad worked in coal mines and on the highways and farmed in Wood County. He freighted with teams in Ward County, farmed at different times in Jones, Baylor, and Knox Counties, and returned later to Wood County and became an independent trucker in the 1930s.

Years after the death of her mother, Grandmother found herself with a brood of four half-brothers near the ages of her own three oldest sons. She is said to have stated many times, "If it were not for my brothers, I could do a better job with my own boys."

I saw the reactions of those half-brothers when she passed away and am convinced she did a good job with the whole pack.

NICHOLSON, CARL H. Interviewed October 22, 1999, Garland.

Born on December 6, 1908, in Bee County, Carl Nicholson remembers scraping early morning snow from outdoor privy seats. Fortunately he lived in South Texas through much of his childhood, so those mornings were rare. He is one of those few remaining citizens who rode a horse to school.

Carl was reared in a time when hunting and trapping were still a part of survival. "Maybe we could not properly be classified as pioneers, but the only difference was that the pioneers staked a claim and fought the Indians, and we signed a mortgage and fought to make the payments."

He later mastered the printing trade and spent his working years at many newspapers across the state. He married, raised a family, and enjoys good health at age ninety-one.

Carl spoke of his grandfather Nicholson. "He was about sixty-five when he lost his right leg, and although he learned to use crutches, he was never active afterwards. Grandpa didn't smoke, but he chewed Brown Mule Dark plug tobacco. He wasn't the only one in the family who used tobacco. Uncle Henry was a Star Navy man and Uncle Will favored Thick Tinsley. Uncle Frank rolled cigarettes with Prince Albert, and Uncle Ed rolled Bull Durham. Dad did not smoke or chew."

Nicholson talked about how hard another grandparent, Mary Ann Atkins, worked. "When Grandma did rest she would relax with a dip of snuff on the frazzled end of a hackberry twig. She called the twig her 'tooth brush' and enjoyed it while she sat in a rocking chair beside a window. While she was seated there she would be tatting or sewing quilt pieces together."

Carl witnessed the birth of the automobile and the airplane and at various times in his life owned not only a Hupmobile, but also a Terraplane.

NORRIS, PARKS. Interviewed 1950, Goree.

Born in 1898, Parks grew up following in the footsteps of a self-taught father who was a cowboy and a doctor of animals. He learned both trades well and was the one called when work required the best of either skill. In charge of the city water services of a small West Texas town for many years during my youth, Parks spent much of his time guiding and reining in his son, Jimmy, and I. He spared no effort in seeing that we followed a productive path.

"When a couple of young guys get a reputation of being a little wild, everything in the county is laid on them," he once mentioned to the pair of us.

Parks may have excused us when he should have busted us. Maybe he understood how much rope to give a colt, but with the aid of others and a brother-in-law county sheriff who later became a Texas Ranger, he, like the old cowman said, kept us "free of the pen and out of the legislature."

Parks, the master of understatement, was also the type of cowboy others called on to catch their mounts. An expert at throwing a rope with an underhand, remuda loop, rising from the ground, Mr. Norris returned to the ranch life before his death in 1954.

PARTLOW, W. E., deceased. Excerpts from Fred Arrington and others, *A History of Dickens County*, Nortex Publications Inc., 1971.

Born in 1872, Partlow, "the Pitchfork Kid," was found a lonely orphan wandering through the streets of Kansas City in 1884 by "Uncle" Ridge Greathouse. The waif, a fearful boy with a strong desire to be a cowboy, was deposited by Greathouse in the care of D.B. Gardner, ranch manager for the Pitchfork spread in Dickens County, Texas. Ridge made a living at the time by poisoning predatory animals.

According to legend, "the Kid" was orphaned after living with two uncles. The uncles were killed for cattle rustling before the boy accepted Uncle Ridge's (no relation) offer to come to West Texas.

If anyone ever did justice to and reflected the image given to Texas cowboys by early romanticists, legend tells us that person was the handsome Pitchfork Kid. Dressed in city suits, wearing no ornamental device except his self-crafted, multicolored, horsehair watch cord, he is said to have personified all that turn-of-the-century West Texas was about. A cowboy's cowboy and an expert roper, the Kid was a highly trusted man among the hands. He often served as an "out sideman" who rode off into the ranch lands alone to bring back stray calves. The Kid rarely carried a gun, never shot a man, and despite his stern leadership on the range, always helped youngsters eager to learn the trade.

The Kid was critically injured "topping off" a horse for a fellow cowboy on the Pitchfork in 1892. Unconscious for nineteen days and thought to be dying, he was transported to a hospital in Trinidad, Colorado. When the Kid awoke in the Catholic hospital and saw the nurses in their robes, he asked, "Is this Heaven?" He recovered to become one of the great riders of the range and in 1897 won the Old Settlers Reunion Rodeo calf roping at Seymour.

L. M. (Rip) Griffin of Lubbock said, "I feel that he and I had quite a bit in common for I, too, was raised from a dogie."

Mrs. Duff Green said, "My husband first knew the Kid in 1889 at Old Raynor, worked with him through the Pitchfork and Matador ranches."

"Old cowboys who worked for the famed Matador and Pitchfork around the turn of the century remembered Partlow as a pipe-smoking gentleman who shaved whenever possible and always requested a healthy insertion of onions in every plate of food.

"He rode a big saddle with long pockets and prided himself on the aged pale-yellow color of his meershaum pipe. His wide, black mustache was a familiar sight on the ranch lands along the croton breaks, east of Dickens.

"Mr. Partlow moved to New Mexico and shortly after was killed in a fall from a load of hay. It is thought his head struck a rock, but there were no witnesses. Several of his old friends doubted his death was an accident."

Douglas Meador, an authority on Matador cowboy lore, describes his meeting with the Kid as "talking with the most true representative of what a cowboy should be."

PRUITT, MARY LOIS BANKS, deceased. Excerpts from Nina Smith and others, *A History of the Humble, Texas, Area*, D.A.R, 1976.

Mrs. Pruitt's father, Will Banks, was an orphan who witnessed the killing of his own father and a slave as they returned from the Civil War; "the slave carrying Granddad's valise.

"After the murder it was found that a deed to one of the largest lots in Athens (Georgia) was missing. The deed was never recovered.

"Mary Lois was born on April 15, 1888, and raised under the influence of a dearly loved black 'Mammy.' Her life was enriched by early sayings borrowed from this surrogate mother: 'Sit on the table, get married before you're able' or, 'Friday dreamed, Saturday told, come to pass 'fore you're nine days old.'"

Something about the last phrase must have impressed Mary Lois because she added that at age twelve, tagging after older twin brothers, she accepted a bribe of learning to dip snuff for not tattling. By this time her family had moved to Pleasant Mound, Texas. Here she met and married her beloved Henry.

In 1909 the Pruitts traveled to New Mexico in a covered wagon to take up a homestead. Not finding their "pot of gold" they returned to Texas and later in 1917 moved to Humble, Texas, during that area's second oil-boom period.

The Pruitts remained in Humble, raised a family of five, and Mrs. Pruitt was blessed to love and enjoy not only grandchildren, but also great-grandchildren. Faith, charm, and a great sense of humor reflect in her story.

QUIZENBERRY, JOHNNIE (FRITZ), deceased. Excerpts from Josephine Hooper Campbell and other committee members, *Knox County History*, Haskell Free Press, 1966.

Mrs. Johnnie Patton (Fritz) Quizenberry was born January 21, 1910. She taught school at Goree, Texas, for many years. Known for a sense of humor and a devotion to children, she left few dry eyes among her many friends when death called her on July 21, 1997.

REGEN, LAVERN CUMMINS, deceased. Excerpts from Rex A. Felker and others, *Haskell County and Its Pioneers*, Nortex Press, Quanah, 1975.

Born in 1904 in Bell County, Texas, LaVern moved to Haskell with her family in 1907. The daughter of a Haskell doctor, LaVern said, "The lot of a country doctor was hard and uncertain in many ways. Telephones were few and far between. Messages were often relayed, and directions were sometimes sparse. 'Come out past Ballew, Paint Creek, Joe Bailey (or some other rural community) about eight miles. There'll be a lantern hanging on the front gate at the ranch, and the house is about four miles inside the gate.'

"Papa came home and told Mama of a child he'd attended at the wagon yard who was dying. She and Mrs. Tyson went to the yard to see what they could do. The mother had one request. She said that the child had always wanted some shoes, and she wanted him to be buried in shoes. When my mother was killed in a wreck hundreds of miles from home and the residents of the little town of Alice were so kind, I couldn't help remembering the wagon yard incident.

"It seemed to me that bread cast upon the waters sometimes returns in kind."

REYNOLDS, CLEM FRANKLIN "DOC," deceased. Excerpts from Mrs. Clyde Warwick and others, *The Randall County Story*, Pioneer Publishers, Hereford, 1969.

"Doc" was born the seventh of fifteen children at Tioga, Texas, on April 17, 1894. He was named after a great-uncle, Clem J. Rogers, who was the father of the humorist Will Rogers. He married Bess Katherine Myers on Christmas Eve, 1914.

Doc said, "I got my first job away from home at age seventeen. A neighbor got behind on his farming and I went to help him. Every time I went to catch the mules his dog barked and scared them away. I had an ol' thirty-eight Colt, and finally, I got this gun and shot at the dog. I missed the dog and hit the mule. Gosh, I was in a fix, working for $25 a month, and shooting a $200 mule. But, I got lucky and the vet saved the mule. He only charged $20.

"I lived in an ol' shack they had on that place, and the rats nearly carried me off. The grub wasn't too good either. About all I had to eat was rice, sourdough biscuits, and syrup. And the ol' lady complained I ate too much of that. I would cook a dipper full of rice for breakfast and eat the half left over for supper. When I left there, I weighed a hundred and twenty-five pounds."

Mr. Reynolds retired in 1960. His zest for life and good humor evidences itself in his stories.

RYDER, ETHEL GLOVER, deceased. Excerpts from History Commission and others, *Knox County History*, Haskell Free Press, 1966.

Ethel was born in Knox County in 1899. Her father was a cowboy who worked for the Halsell Ranch and in 1910 the Shawyer Ranch. Ethel married Marion E. "Sug" Ryder and after her mother's death raised her younger siblings. She and Marion lived south of Gilliland for many years then moved to California.

SCOTT, S. W., deceased. Excerpts from Rex A. Felker and others, *Haskell County and Its Pioneers*, Nortex Press, Quanah. 1975.

Mr. Scott, accompanied by two other men, arrived in Haskell County on July 9, 1884, driving a herd of over a thousand head of cattle. He fenced, rode out, and settled a "wide-open" country. "After four years of gypsy life, I went back to Georgetown and read law for several months and was admitted to the bar in January 1889. I returned to Haskell, hung out a shingle, and practiced there until 1913."

SPANN, JACK ORVILLE. Interviewed November 22, 1999, Greenville.

Born in 1919 in Denton County, Jack grew into manhood working the fields of Texas before the days of tractors. His family moved to the High Plains of Texas when he was a child then returned to the Denton County area.

Jack married Ruby Leola Laylan in 1942. Serving in the army during the war, he was assigned to the 30th Evacuation Hospital. His group was sent to the South Pacific and attached to the 5th Regiment of the 1st Marines on the island of New Britain. At other times they provided medical services for an Australian outfit as well as for U.S. forces in New Guinea.

Among the many fierce battles the allied forces engaged in during those difficult days was one that sticks in Jack's mind. During the month of January 1944, on the island of New Britain, the Marines were engaged with the Japanese for control of hill 660 on Cape Glouchester. Today, fifty-five years later, a mutual respect for the courage and professionalism shown by both Jack and, at that time, a young Marine warrior of that battle named Harold "Mac" McKenzie, has bloomed into an everlasting friendship. Nudging entry into their early eighties, they share weekly telephone visits and continue to support each other through both good and difficult times.

Jack trained as a railroad fireman and worked at that trade for a short time after serving as an army medic during World War II. Later, like so many of his peers, Jack welcomed the arrival of the mechanization age. He became a sought-after expert in his chosen field of tool and die manufacturing and ended his career as a consultant in that industry.

TAYLOR, L. J. "BEDI." Interviewed July 4, 1980, Colorado City.

Mr. Taylor was born June 22, 1903, in Ennis, Texas. Near Christmas of his fourth year his family moved to Mitchell County. During his youth Bedi worked cattle "a-horseback" when not using his favorite mule Barney. He participated in one of the last sustained cattle drives in that country, helping to move a herd of his father's cattle from drought-stricken Nolan County to shower-freshened pasture at Odessa, Texas.

This drive of approximately 120 miles took place around 1917. Bedi made part of the trip in the wagon after his mount bounced off a mesquite tree. His kneecap, dislocated by the impact, pointed the wrong direction. Occurring on the third day of the drive, he was soon back in the saddle.

After marriage, Mr. Taylor took a job in a hardware store that he later bought. Interested in all things modern and anxious to learn new ways, Bedi took courses from the University of Texas and soon enjoyed a reputation of being able to fix anything electric, primarily radios. It was an exciting time for him, with electricity revolutionizing the rolling plains.

George H. Mahon, chairman of the Committee on House Appropriations for many years, was a close childhood and lifelong friend of Mr. Taylor. Bedi delighted in telling of his experiences traveling with George and managing the sound equipment used in the representative's initial campaign for the House in 1934. A humble man, Mr. Taylor was proud of his friend's success in Washington as "the third most powerful man in the United States."

World War II scorched the earth, and soon Bedi's reputation with things electrical prompted a hard decision. He was too old for the draft. A group of officers visited him at his store and asked him to take a commission and serve in military communications and radar.

Mr. Taylor struggled with the decision and ultimately refused it, but not the request to serve mankind. At the age of eighty-five and on his deathbed in 1988, while I held an unlit Travis Club cigar to his lips, he asked, "What is man's last duty to his fellow man?"

I remembered him discussing how moving he'd found his Masonic training. I recalled the thousands of individual silver dollars he'd given children and others in need of a grin. I thought of how frequently his wife was startled to learn of anonymous charities he'd performed on a limited budget. I wondered at a man sitting silently with a friend in his church's basement each Sunday for fifty-five years counting the offering. I remembered the small container of cup-grease he bought from a newly married school teaching son-in-law who moonlighted at a second job on a quiet Sunday afternoon. I found the grease, bought as a token, in his garage after his death. It sits today, unopened after forty-two years.

I'm sure my answer was inadequate.

WELLS, CHARLEY, deceased. Excerpt from Rex A. Felker and others, *Haskell County and Its Pioneers*, Nortex Press, Quanah, 1975.

Charley Wells, a citizen of Haskell, Texas, was born September 12, 1886, in Montgomery County, Texas. Charley soldiered in the 824th Transportation Corps during World War I and had the dubious distinction of being stationed in France. This was back in the days when the army was segregated, and the chant of the American Doughboy was: "Kaiser Bill went up the hill, to take a look at France. Kaiser Bill came down the hill with bullets in his pants."

In 1975, still alert, Charley recalled that General "Blackjack Pershing" commanded the American Expeditionary Forces, and he (Charley) was up for corporal when the Armistice was signed. Haskell's citizens stated in their county history, "He justly deserves a proud salute of honor from all citizens for the many years of service he devoted to his country and his fellow man. When he reached eighty-nine, his friends hoped for him many more birthdays and wished him 'At ease, old soldier.'"

Other Book References

(Alphabetical listing of individuals from reference sources followed by text bibliography)

(Alexander, F. G.), Felker, Rex A. and others, *Haskell County and Its Pioneers*, Nortex Press, Quanah, Texas, 1975.

(Allen, Walter), Historical Committee, *A Stake in the Prairie*, Taylor Publishing Co. Dallas, 1984.

(Arnecke, Dr.), Dewitt County Historical Commission, *The History of Dewitt County Texas*, Curtis Media Inc., 1991.

(Barrow, Clyde), E. R. Milner, *The Lives and Times of Bonnie and Clyde*, Southern Illinois University Press, 1996.

(Bates, John), The Knox County History Committee, *Knox County History*, Haskell Free Press, 1966.

(Beach, Mr. & Mrs.), Wylie, Rosa Lee and others, *History of Van Horn and Culberson County*, Pioneer Book Publishers, Hereford, 1973.

(Bender, Jody), Tarpley, Fred, *Jefferson: Riverport to the Southwest*, Eakin Press, Austin, Texas, 1983.

(Blizzard, Dickens County), Fred Arrington and others, *A History of Dickens County*, Nortex Publications Inc., Quanah, 1971.

(Browning, G. L.), Warwick, Mrs. Clyde W. and others, *The Randall County Story*, Pioneer Book Publishers, Hereford, Texas, 1969.

("Bub," T Anchor cowboy), ibid.

(Burns, Willie), McComb David G., *Galveston: A History*, University of Texas Press, Austin, Texas, 1986.

(DeWitt County), Dewitt County Historical Commission, *The History of Dewitt County Texas*, Curtis Media Inc., 1991.

(Casey, Mrs. C. Parks), and others, *The Life and Lives of Brown County People*, The Brown County Historical Society, 1987.

(Cooks, H. T.), The Knox County History Committee, *Knox County History*, Haskell Free Press, 1966.

(Cousins, Sheriff Al), Felker, Rex A. and others, *Haskell County and Its Pioneers*, Nortex Press, Quanah, Texas, 1975.

(Cummins, Dr., by LaVern Cummins), ibid.

(Cummings Gordon, Mrs. Charles), Warwick, Mrs. Clyde W. and others, *The Randall County Story*, Pioneer Book Publishers, Hereford, Texas, 1969.

(Dallas, WPA Guide), Dallas Public Library, *The WPA Dallas Guide and History*, University of Texas Press, 1992.

(Dannell, Frank P.), Tarpley, Fred, *Jefferson; Riverport to the Southwest*, Eakin Press, Austin, Texas, 1983.

(Felker, Rex A.), Felker, Rex A. and others, *Haskell County and Its Pioneers*, Nortex Press, Quanah, 1975.

(Fires, Dickens County), Fred Arrington and others, *A History of Dickens County*, Nortex Publications Inc., Quanah, 1971.

(Gilliland residents), The Knox County History Committee, *Knox County History*, Haskell Free Press, 1966.

(Goeth, Lottilie Fuchs), Lottilie Goeth, *Memoirs of a Texas Grandmother*, Eakin Press, Burnet, 1982.

(Goode, Mrs. John "Dicie" Turner), The Knox County History Committee, *Knox County History*, Haskell Free Press, 1966.

(Green, Mrs. Duff), Fred Arrington and others, *A History of Dickens County*, Nortex Publications Inc., Quanah, 1971.

(Harvey, George), ibid.

(Haskell County historians), Felker, Rex A. and others, *Haskell County and Its Pioneers*, Nortex Press, Quanah, 1975.

(Holland, Judge), *History of Potter County*, Nortex Publications. Quanah, Wichita Falls, Texas, 1972.

(Horn, Elder R. C.), Stambaugh, J. Lee and Lilliand J. and the State Historical Association, *A History of Collin County*, Lund Press Inc., Minneapolis, Minnesota, 1958.

(Howeth, Poly Archer), Smith, Nina Sheffield and others, *A History of the Humble, Texas, Area*, Humble, Texas, 1976.

(Kempner, Harris), McComb, David G., *Galveston: A History*, University of Texas Press, Austin, Texas, 1986.

(Key, Della Tyler), *History of Potter County*, Nortex Publications. Quanah, Wichita Falls, Texas, 1972.

(Kirkendoll, Eustace), Zachry, Juanita Daniel, *A History of Rural Taylor County*. Nortex Press, Burnet, Texas, 1980.

(Lindley, Mary), ibid.

(Lyons, Captain R. C.), ibid.

(Marshall, Sheriff Schulyer Jr.), Historical Committee, *A Stake in the Prairie*, Taylor Publishing Co., Dallas,1984.

(McHan, Josephine Spain), The County Historical Society and others, *The Life and Lives of Brown County People*, The Brown County Historical Society, 1987.

(McClin, Dorthy), Smith, Nina Sheffield and others, *A History of the Humble, Texas, Area*, Humble, Texas, 1976.

(Mesquite, First National Bank), Historical Committee, *A Stake in the Prairie*, Taylor Publishing Co., Dallas, 1984.

(Mesquite, Texas historians), ibid.

(Moody, Colonel W. G.), McComb, David G., *Galveston: A History*, University of Texas Press, Austin, 1986.

(Moore, Harvey), Tarpley, Fred, *Jefferson: Riverport to the Southwest*, Eakin Press, Austin, 1983.

(Panic of 1907), Historical Committee, *A Stake in the Prairie*, Taylor Publishing Co., Dallas, 1984.

(Partlow, W. E.), Fred Arrington and others, *A History of Dickens County*, Nortex Publications Inc., Quanah, Texas, 1971.

(Patton, Mrs. Johnny), The Knox County History Committee, *Knox County History*, Haskell Free Press, 1966.

(Phillips, Mrs. W. P. "Elizabeth"), ibid.

(Pierson, Alfred and Marshall), Felker, Rex A. and others, *Haskell County and Its Pioneers*, Nortex Press, Quanah, Texas, 1975.

(Randall County historians), Warwick, Mrs. Clyde W. and others, *The Randall County Story*, Pioneer Book Publishers, Hereford, Texas, 1969.

(Regen, LaVern Cummins), Felker, Rex A. and others, *Haskell County and Its Pioneers*, Nortex Press, Quanah, Texas, 1975.

(Reynolds, Clem "Doc"), Warwick, Mrs. Clyde W. and others, *The Randall County Story*, Pioneer Book Publishers, Hereford, Texas, 1969.

(Rochester residents), Felker, Rex A. and others, *Haskell County and Its Pioneers*, Nortex Press, Quanah, Texas, 1975.

(Russell, Charles), Russell, Charles M., *Trails Plowed Under*, Doubleday & Co., New York, 1946.

(Ryder, Ethel Glover), The Knox County History Committee, *Knox County History*, Haskell Free Press, 1966.

(Scott, M. S.), Felker, Rex A. and others, *Haskell County and Its Pioneers*, Nortex Press, Quanah, Texas, 1975.

(Sheffield, Hayne), James Tull chapter of the D.A.R., Nina Sheffield and others, *A History of the Humble, Texas, Area*, 1976.

(Short, Velma Nichols), Rains County Historical Commission, *History of Rains County*, County Historical Commission, Emory, Texas, 1980.

(Spain, Levi Anderson), Laughlin, Hochhalter and others, *The Life and Lives of Brown County People*, The Brown County Historical Society, 1987.

(Spain, Mrs. Lizzie Owen), ibid.

(Price, Turner), The Knox County History Committee, *Knox County History*, Haskell Free Press, 1966.

(Propps, Jack), ibid.

(Van Zandt County), Hall, Elizabeth Margaret, *A History of Van Zandt County*, Jenkins Publishing Co., Austin, 1976.

(Villa, Franscisco "Pancho"), The Presidio County Historical Commission, *A History of Marfa and Presido County, Vol. 11*, Nortex Press, Austin, 1985.

(Warren, Robert L.), Historical Committee, *A Stake in the Prairie*, Taylor Publishing Co., Dallas, 1984.

("Whiskey the Road to Ruin"), Felker, Rex A. and others, *Haskell County and Its Pioneers*, Nortex Press, Quanah, Texas, 1975.

(Wolves, Dickens County), Fred Arrington and others, *A History of Dickens County*, Nortex Publications Inc., Quanah, Texas, 1971.

(Wylie, Rosa Lee), Wylie, Rosa Lee and others, *History of Van Horn and Culberson County*, Pioneer Book Publishers, Hereford, Texas, 1973.

Index